P9-CKQ-829

Studies in Immersion Education

THE LANGUAGE AND EDUCATION LIBRARY

Series Editor
Professor David Corson, *The Ontario Institute for Studies in Education,
252 Bloor St. West, Toronto, Ontario, Canada M5S 1V6*

Other Books in the Series

Competing and Consensual Voices
    PATRICK COSTELLO and SALLY MITCHELL (eds)
Critical Theory and Classroom Talk
    ROBERT YOUNG
Language Policies in English-Dominant Countries
    MICHAEL HERRIMAN and BARBARA BURNABY (eds)
Language Policy Across the Curriculum
    DAVID CORSON
Language, Minority Education and Gender
    DAVID CORSON
Learning about Punctuation
    NIGEL HALL and ANNE ROBINSON (eds)
Making Multicultural Education Work
    STEPHEN MAY
School to Work Transition in Japan
    KAORI OKANO
Reading Acquisition Processes
    G.B. THOMPSON, W.E. TUNMER and T. NICHOLSON (eds)
Worlds of Literacy
    M. HAMILTON, D. BARTON and R. IVANIC (eds)

Other Books of Interest

The Age Factor in Second Language Acquistion
    D. SINGLETON and Z. LENGYEL (eds)
Foundations of Bilingual Education and Bilingualism
    COLIN BAKER
The Good Language Learner
    N. NAIMAN, M. FRÖHLICH, H. H. STERN and A. TODESCO
A Parents' and Teachers' Guide to Bilingualism
    COLIN BAKER
Policy and Practices in Bilingual Education
    O. GARCÍA and C. BAKER (eds)
Second Language Practice
    GEORGES DUQUETTE (ed.)

Please contact us for the latest book information:
Multilingual Matters Ltd, Frankfurt Lodge, Clevedon Hall,
Victoria Road, Clevedon BS21 7SJ, UK

448
D330

THE LANGUAGE AND EDUCATION LIBRARY 11
Series Editor: Professor David J. Corson
The Ontario Institute for Studies in Education

Studies in Immersion Education

Ellen

Elaine M. Day and Stan M. Shapson

G

WITHDRAWN

MULTILINGUAL MATTERS LTD
Clevedon • Philadelphia • Adelaide

LIBRARY ST. MARY'S COLLEGE

To Rod Day and Kate Shapson

Library of Congress Cataloging in Publication Data

Day, Elaine Mellen
Studies in Immersion Education/Elaine M. Day and Stan Shapson
The Language and Education Library: 11
Includes bibliographical references and index
1. French language–Study and teaching–British Columbia. 2. French
language–Study and teaching–Immersion method. I. Shapson, Stan.
II. Title. III. Series
PC2068.B75D39   1996
448'.007'0711–dc20   95-49679

British Library Cataloguing in Publication Data

A CIP catalogue record for this book is available from the British Library.

ISBN 1-85359-356-7 (hbk)
ISBN 1-85359-355-9 (pbk)

Multilingual Matters Ltd

UK: Frankfurt Lodge, Clevedon Hall, Victoria Road, Clevedon BS21 7SJ.
USA: 1900 Frost Road, Suite 101, Bristol, PA 19007, USA.
Australia: P.O. Box 6025, 95 Gilles Street, Adelaide, SA 5000, Australia.

Copyright © 1996 Elaine M. Day and Stan M. Shapson

All rights reserved. No part of this work may be reproduced in any form or by
any means without permission in writing from the publisher.

Typeset by Bookcraft, Stroud, Glos.
Printed and bound in Great Britain by WBC Book Manufacturers Ltd.

Contents

Acknowledgements

Many capable and dedicated groups and individuals have cooperated with and assisted us in our research. They are acknowledged in the individual reports and articles which form the basis for the various chapters in this book. Here we would simply like to reiterate a hearty thank you to all groups and individuals for the assistance and support so generously provided. We would especially like to express our appreciation to Marie-Claude Collins and Florence Rioux for their cooperation in designing the experimental materials (Chapter 2), Claudette Tardif for her cooperation in the study of teacher education (Chapter 5), and Josette Desquins for her collaboration in the studies of teacher education and professional development (Chapters 5 and 6).

We are grateful to Simon Fraser University and York University for their cooperation and support. We would also like to acknowledge the following funding and contracting agencies for the financial support which made the studies possible: British Columbia Ministry of Education (Chapters 1 and 3); Social Sciences and Humanities Research Council of Canada (Chapters 2 and 5); the Department of Canadian Heritage and the Canadian Association of Immersion Teachers (Chapter 6).

We would sincerely like to thank Thokozile B. Kheswa for her excellent research and editorial assistance and Claire Budin for her careful preparation of the final manuscript.

Our special gratitude is reserved for our long-time associate, Lynn Reader, who carried major administrative and secretarial responsibilities and was an indispensable member of our research team for many years.

Introduction

A new era in second language education began to unfold in Canada with the enacting of the Official Languages Act in 1969. Through this act, Canada adopted an official policy of bilingualism, with French gaining equal rights and status with English in Parliament and in all services of the Federal Government. This led to a major effort by the government to promote and stimulate instruction in the two official languages. At the same time, the public – in particular, English-speaking parents – were expressing concerns about the low levels of competence in French being attained by their children, even after 12 years of schooling. Faced with the growing importance of bilingualism and the apparent ineffectiveness of existing instructional methods for French second language (FSL), anglophone parents began a grassroots movement to consider alternatives. This led to a major Canadian innovation in second languages, immersion education, which has since taken root in many countries.

Immersion is very different from what had been the prevailing traditional second language approach with French taught as one subject in the school curriculum for a short period of time each day. Immersion involves an intensive language approach with a switch of languages between the home and the school. Initially all or at least a very significant part of the curriculum is taught using the children's second language (French) as the language of instruction. Explicit French language teaching is not necessarily excluded from the immersion classroom. However, the distinguishing feature of immersion is that students learn language primarily through subject matter rather than by formal language teaching (e.g. Genesee, 1987; Stern, 1978).

The program's main aims and its pedagogical and sociological characteristics have been described elsewhere (Genesee, 1983). French immersion is a voluntary program designed for majority language students who speak English, the predominant language of the school and community. This context for second language learning should be carefully distinguished from that which applies to minority language students whose native

1

language (and the language predominantly spoken in the home) is not the same as the language used by the school (Shapson, 1984).

Extensive research has been conducted on immersion programs across Canada. The findings consistently demonstrate positive outcomes: students achieve high levels of proficiency in their second language (French); there is no long-term cost to their progress in their first language (English) or other school subjects; and they display positive attitudes toward French language and culture (e.g. Shapson & Day, 1982, 1988 in British Columbia; Lapkin et al., 1991 and Swain & Lapkin, 1982 in Ontario; Genesee, 1978, 1984 and Lambert & Tucker, 1972 in Québec; Gray, 1986 in New Brunswick).

The immersion program has grown considerably since the mid 1960s when it started as a pilot project in one school in the French-speaking province of Québec. Influenced largely by parental pressures and demands, Federal policy and support, and extensive documentation of the program's effectiveness, immersion is now provided in all ten provinces and two territories of Canada and enrolls over 300,000 students (Commissioner of Official Languages, 1995). In British Columbia, Canada's most westerly province, enrollment is over 30,000 students and represents approximately 5% of the student population (British Columbia Ministry of Education, 1995).

Of particular interest is the growth of immersion education internationally (Genesee, 1987; Rebuffot, 1993). In the United States, immersion programs are reported in 25 states (Center for Applied Linguistics, 1993). Various forms of immersion education are also operating world-wide (Artigal, 1991; Bostwick, 1994; Buss & Laurén, 1995; Clyne, 1991; de Courcy, 1993; Laurén & Vesterbacka, 1990; Rebuffot, 1993; Johnson & Swain, in press). These vary with respect to starting age and amount of instructional time in the second language and are implemented for diverse reasons – for example, enrichment as in Sweden, language revival and retention as in Wales, and to promote an official language as in Catalonia.

Overview of the Book

This book presents a unique collection of research studies we have conducted from our base as a research team in British Columbia, Canada. Our work focuses on three broad areas: program evaluation and assessment; curriculum and instruction; and teacher education. It is intended to serve as a resource for educators interested in gaining information about the impact of immersion on educational policy, student outcomes, second language curriculum and teacher education. While every sociocultural context is unique and the dangers of generalizing from findings gained in one social and educational setting to another are well recognized (Baker, 1993a), systematic research can serve as a useful point of reference and comparison for educators across different settings. This collection of research studies will be informative to those involved in immersion education in Canada and beyond.

Because of its experimental nature, French immersion has been the subject of numerous evaluations since its inception. Many studies were conducted for individual school districts during the early years of the program and mainly involved standardized norm-referenced tests for monitoring student performance. In Section 1, we provide a narrative account of our experiences in developing a systematic approach to *evaluation and assessment* in the province of British Columbia. We trace the evolution of evaluation from initial studies commissioned by individual school districts when the program was first introduced to more recent province-wide studies conducted as the program came to be more firmly established as a viable alternative within the regular school system. Because of the growth of immersion education in North America and internationally, there is a need for information on methods, models, and issues in large-scale program evaluation. For example, one needs to be concerned about: particularly difficult areas to measure such as oral proficiency skills; using assessment data to shed light on factors which can lead to program improvement; and ways in which assessment of alternative second language programs can interface with large-scale assessment models developed for mainstream programs.

In Section 2, we focus on *curriculum and instruction* for immersion. Because research results show that immersion students have highly developed communicative abilities in French but lag behind in grammar, many immersion educators identify improving students' grammatical competence as a major priority and call for curriculum research to determine how best to accomplish this. In Chapter 2, we present an experimental study to stimulate grammatical teaching in French immersion classrooms. The study is based on second language curriculum theory, which seeks to combine less formal, experiential teaching, involving the natural, unanalyzed use of language with more formal language teaching based on analysis and practice of the linguistic code (Allen, 1983; Stern, 1982, 1992).

A critical feature of French immersion as a model of second language teaching is the integration of content or subject matter teaching with language teaching aims. Surprisingly, little empirical information is available on how immersion teachers go about their dual role of promoting language and subject matter learning. In Chapter 3, we discuss language and subject matter integration, based on case studies of French immersion classrooms. The case studies yield valuable descriptive data on immersion teachers' beliefs and practices and can serve as a catalyst for teachers to examine their own strategies and practices with respect to language/subject matter integration.

Immersion educators are increasingly calling for more systematic planning for language development to improve students' second language competence (e.g. Lyster, 1987, 1990; Snow et al., 1989). In Chapter 4, we explore some of the questions and issues that should be considered in addressing this need. These include meeting the program's dual goals, weighing the importance of language teaching in immersion, maintaining a balanced view of communicative proficiency, attending to the implicit language curriculum, and keeping in mind the social and psychological nature of language learning.

The focus of Section 3 addresses *teachers and their education*. The rapid growth of French immersion in Canada brought with it an unfulfilled demand for specialized teaching personnel and a need to design new teacher education programs to prepare teachers for the demanding challenges of teaching a second language and teaching subject matter through this language. In a research agenda for immersion for the 1990s, teacher education was singled out for critical attention (Lapkin et al., 1990) – a recurring theme of immersion researchers internationally (Artigal, 1991; Bernhardt & Schrier, 1992; Clyne, 1991; MacNeil, 1994). How are teacher education institutions responding to the challenge? In Chapter 5, we present an in-depth examination of immersion teacher education in two institutions in Western Canada. We focus on the clientele for these programs, the models on which the programs are based, participants' experiences and needs, and future educational planning; and we analyze the programs in relation to current research on teacher education. Next we turn attention to immersion teachers' perceptions of their role and needs for support and improvement. We discuss in Chapter 6 the major findings and conclusions of a national survey of the professional development needs of French immersion teachers, which we conducted under commission to a national professional organization, the Canadian Association of Immersion Teachers.

Our research goes well beyond a focus on student outcomes of second language learning and interweaves important perspectives for large-scale assessment, curriculum and instruction, and teacher education. We complete the book with a summary of our work, followed by concluding comments and future directions for immersion programs.

1 Program Evaluation and Student Assessment in British Columbia: A Narrative Account

Introduction

French immersion has been the subject of numerous evaluations since its inception. Because of the experimental nature of the immersion program, parents, educators, and the public at large wanted assurances that children suffered no harm to their progress in their first language (English) or academic subjects. There was also considerable interest in assessing the French language skills of immersion students to determine the degree of bilingualism that could be attained by introducing this new program option in the schools. At the same time, the Canadian government, while actively promoting bilingualism and providing funding directly to provincial governments for innovative and experimental language programs, required evaluation for accountability purposes.

In this chapter, we provide a narrative account of our experiences with developing a systematic approach to evaluation of immersion in the province of British Columbia.[1] We trace the evolution of evaluation from initial studies commissioned by individual school districts when the program was first introduced in the early 1970s to recent province-wide studies conducted as the program became firmly established as a viable alternative within the regular school system.

Starting the Evaluation Process

Across Canada, as school districts began to respond to parental pressure to introduce immersion programs, they characteristically involved university researchers in conducting evaluations of their pilot programs. During the 1970s, as a research team based at Simon Fraser University in the Vancouver area, British Columbia, we were frequently called on by individual school districts to undertake this task. Specifically, we were asked to address the major questions policymakers and the public had of this bold new initiative: What are the effects of the program on students' English language development, on their academic achievement, and on their attainment of bilingual language skills?

As was the case with other evaluation studies of this period in Canada, we used standardized norm-referenced tests to measure linguistic progress and academic subject matter achievement. From a research perspective, it was important to compare the effects of program alternatives which differed on factors such as entry level and amount of instructional time in French and to assess the effectiveness of immersion in different settings (Genesee, 1987; Shapson & Kaufman, 1978; Swain, 1978). It was also important to gain information on the relative performance of immersion students vis-à-vis native French-speaking students as well as students enrolled in more traditional French second language programs.

For testing students' achievement in English and mathematics, we commonly used the Canadian Tests of Basic Skills (Nelson Canada), a standardized test normed on English-speaking students across Canada. This allowed us to monitor the progress of immersion students with that of comparison groups of regular English program students.

For assessing French, it quickly became apparent that tests developed for students in traditional French second language (FSL) programs were not appropriate to measure the rapidly developing language skills of immersion students and therefore native francophones were used as a reference group. We selected a series of standardized French language arts tests normed on francophone students in Québec (Tests de Rendement en Français) and listening comprehension tests developed by researchers in Ontario (e.g. Barik, 1975, 1978). These tests were also used in evaluation studies of immersion programs elsewhere in Canada, so that we had data from other French immersion programs with which to compare the British Columbia students. Suitable measures of French speaking and writing were not available, nor were district budgetary funds sufficient for undertaking the labor-intensive task of examining these skills.

Wherever possible, we used a quasi-experimental design in the district studies and compared immersion students' progress with that of selected control groups of students in the regular English program. The limitations when researchers have no choice but to use non-randomized assignment of groups are widely acknowledged (Carey, 1984; Genesee, 1987; Swain &

Lapkin, 1982). The results of the individual district studies we undertook confirmed the results of evaluation studies elsewhere in Canada, showing no harm to students' progress in English or academic subjects and considerable progress in French language skills (e.g. Lambert & Tucker, 1972; Swain & Lapkin, 1982). At this time, however, it was becoming apparent that the scope of evaluation of immersion would have to broaden.

Broadening the Scope of Evaluation

With the rapid expansion of immersion in the early 1980s, providing evaluation services on a district by district basis became difficult to manage. Districts had only limited funds for evaluation, making it difficult to conduct comprehensive studies, to develop new measures for testing French, and to extend evaluation activities to include investigation of factors which would assist in program development. Some districts were interested in more comprehensive work which could go beyond student outcomes and be more longitudinal in nature. In fact, in one district, we were following cohorts of students from their entry in the program in kindergarten through graduation in grade 12 (Shapson & Kaufman, 1978; Shapson & Day, 1982).

With the positive results from evaluation, confidence in the program grew and the label of 'experimental' began to be lifted. Interest centered more fully on investigating strengths and weaknesses in students' French language competence, particularly in oral proficiency, which was one of the main program goals. A major constraint was the lack of suitable instruments for measuring speaking and other functional areas of French language development and for assessing students' achievement in relation to provincial curricular goals.

We therefore developed an evaluation plan which would combine the continuing needs of individual districts for basic information on their program's effectiveness with the need for more comprehensive information on a province-wide level. A proposal based on this plan was submitted to the provincial government. The scope of the project included oral test development; the collection of normative data on grades 3 and 7 students' French language skills; and surveys of parents, teachers, and administrators. It also included preparation of a self-evaluation package containing instruments, procedures, and provincial data designed to help districts conduct their own evaluations with little outside assistance in subsequent years. This approach, which we had used successfully in previous studies of traditional FSL programs in the province (Shapson, 1982), is consistent with a monitoring and tailoring approach to evaluation (e.g. Cooley, 1983).

In order to conduct a comprehensive study of communicative language skills, we developed a group test of French speaking for grade 3 immersion students (Day & Shapson, 1983, 1987). In addition, we surveyed parents teachers, and administrators to gain contextual information about the program and their opinions and perceptions on issues affecting program development and implementation, such as, availability and access to immersion, optimum conditions for French language development, teacher preparation and in-service (Day & Shapson, 1983; Shapson & Day, 1984). The gathering of contextual information is an important component sometimes found lacking in immersion research (Burns, 1986). This project led to the next phase in our work in which we collaborated with the Ministry to design an approach linking the evaluation of immersion with the ongoing provincial assessment of English programs. This included further work in developing provincial instruments and assessing French language skills (French reading and speaking tests) and in designing a methodology for assessing immersion students' performance on provincial domain-referenced tests in English (reading, mathematics and science).

Provincial Assessment Model: Designing Room for Immersion

For the mainstream English program, a provincial assessment model had been firmly in place to monitor student learning and to provide accountability information to the public and formative information which could be used by the province, districts and schools to maintain strengths and overcome identified weaknesses (Mussio & Greer, 1980). Student outcome and attitude data are collected in one subject area each year for grades 4, 7 and 10. Domain-referenced curriculum tests geared to provincial curricular objectives are developed for each assessment, and contextual information is gathered through teacher questionnaires.

French immersion students were routinely included in the provincial assessments beginning with English reading in 1984, followed by mathematics in 1985 and science in 1986. However, achievement results for immersion students participating in these three assessments were not reported by the Ministry.

By this time, immersion programs had spread to nearly half of the school districts in the province. As well, immersion students were moving through to the intermediate and secondary grades. Given this critical mass, it was important that immersion be included as a legitimate part of the provincial assessment and accountability scheme. For this reason, we worked with the Ministry of Education to incorporate immersion into the provincial assessment model in ways that would allow the unique needs of the program to be addressed. We undertook to design a provincial prototype assessment for immersion with the following objectives: (1) to examine the extent to which students are achieving provincial curricular goals in French reading, listening and speaking; (2) to determine student attitudes toward various aspects of French language and culture and their self-perceptions of their knowledge of French; and (3) to compare immersion students' achievement in previous provincial assessments of English reading, mathematics and science with the achievement of students enrolled in regular English programs. This represented the first attempt by the province to utilize the provincial assessment model with special programs such as French immersion and was an important step, as it further legitimized French immersion as an established educational alternative within the public school system.

Where appropriate, the structure of the assessment mirrored that of provincial assessments in the regular English stream (see Figure 1.1(a)–(e)).

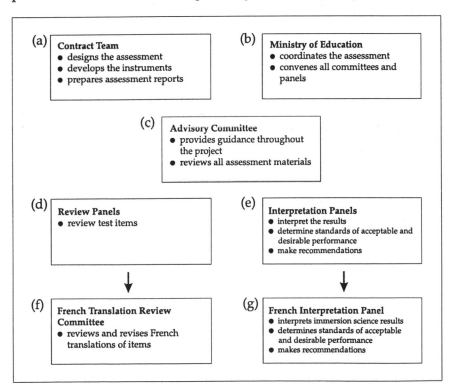

(a) **Contract Team**
• designs the assessment
• develops the instruments
• prepares assessment reports

(b) **Ministry of Education**
• coordinates the assessment
• convenes all committees and panels

(c) **Advisory Committee**
• provides guidance throughout the project
• reviews all assessment materials

(d) **Review Panels**
• review test items

(e) **Interpretation Panels**
• interpret the results
• determine standards of acceptable and desirable performance
• make recommendations

(f) **French Translation Review Committee**
• reviews and revises French translations of items

(g) **French Interpretation Panel**
• interprets immersion science results
• determines standards of acceptable and desirable performance
• makes recommendations

Figure 1.1 Provincial assessment model

Two major bodies assume responsibility for different aspects of the assessment. The Ministry's Student Assessment Branch coordinates the assessment and convenes all committees and panels. A university-based Contract Team (in this case, the authors) designs the assessment, develops all instruments and prepares reports. An Advisory Committee, composed of teachers and administrators from across the province, provides guidance and reviews survey materials. Review Panels, made up of practising teachers, review proposed test items and materials; and Interpretation Panels, representative groups of educators and lay persons, determine standards of acceptable and desirable performance and identify areas of strength and weakness as indicated by the assessment results. This particular feature of the assessment is important for immersion because, as described previously, much of the earlier research was limited to standardized tests comparing immersion students' progress to outside groups, thereby providing a limited base for the interpretation of findings.

Assessing French language skills for immersion

This phase of our work allowed for developing domain-referenced French reading tests and a group test of French speaking for the higher grades.

French reading

As the first step to developing the French reading tests, we met with the provincial Advisory Committee who examined and prioritized objectives from provincial curriculum guides. Next we developed a Table of Specifications based on their recommendations and worked with a team of immersion teachers to select reading passages and test items. The Advisory Committee and Review Panels of immersion teachers reviewed all items.

Following preparation and piloting of two pilot-test forms for each grade, we prepared the final test forms which covered the following five domains: vocabulary; literal comprehension; inferential comprehension; critical comprehension; and graphic materials. A variety of passages were selected; these included poetry, fictional prose, material from social studies texts, functional material such as game instructions and posters, and graphic materials such as maps, graphs and cartoons.

After the data had been collected and analyzed, the Interpretation Panels rated student performance on the five reading domains. Overall, the results indicated that immersion students made good progress in French reading, with the mean scores for most domains falling in the 60–75% range and all Interpretation Panel ratings being Satisfactory or higher. While the results showed that students performed reasonably well in the context of current expectations, they also suggested that there is ample room for growth, in particular, in vocabulary and inferential and critical comprehension, as all groups performed less well in these than in the other two domains (i.e. literal comprehension and graphic materials). Detailed results and recommendations for programmatic improvement can be found in the final report (Day *et al.*, 1988) and subsequent publications (Day & Shapson, 1989).

French speaking

We developed a French speaking test (Day *et al.*, 1987) to elicit speech reflecting a wide variety of language functions (Shafer *et al.*, 1983; Tough, 1977) and to preserve as much as possible the essential features of language use (e.g. interaction-based, unpredictability, purpose) as described by Morrow (1979) in discussing communicative language testing. It is a group test for grade 7 students and is composed of three oral tasks based on a town planning activity: planning of the town; composition of a chain story; and interview. As reported previously (Day & Shapson, 1987, 1989), the group format provides several advantages, especially with respect to the psychological and communicative aspects of testing. For example, it helps minimize testing anxiety and allows opportunities for interaction among testees and between examiner and testees and enables us to elicit both individual and group data. This format has been proposed for testing adults in academic contexts (Folland & Robertson, 1976; Morrison & Lee, 1985), but it still enjoys only limited use and is rarely reported on for testing young second language learners, despite the growing importance of collaborative learning in second language classrooms (Johnson, 1994).

Native French speakers rated the speaking samples on a series of four-point scales designed to measure both the linguistic (e.g. pronunciation) and communicative (e.g. quality of discussion) dimensions of speech. Detailed error analyses were also conducted of the children's correctness in the use of verbs in the story and interview tasks and of their grammar in the town planning task.

Overall, grade 7 immersion students performed well in French speaking. They were able to engage in fairly complex discussions requiring them to use French for a range of purposes, and they did so with ease and enjoyment. The immersion students were not comparable to a group of native French-speaking students in their pronunciation/intonation and oral grammar. However, except for fluency, they were comparable on the more communicative measures (e.g. quality of information, quality of description). Detailed error analyses are available which highlight students' strengths and weaknesses and provide guidelines for curricular and pedagogical strategies to improve the program (Day *et al.*, 1988; Day & Shapson, 1989).

Assessing subject matter achievement in English

It is recalled that in our earlier work we used standardized tests to assess the English language skills and subject matter achievement of immersion students. Because of the need for information on the extent to which immersion students were achieving the objectives specified in provincial curriculum guides dealing with English and subject matter achievement, we developed an approach to include an analysis of immersion students' performance on previous provincial assessments of English reading and other subjects.

We prepared guidelines for school superintendents of all participating school districts, enabling them to select a comparison school in the regular English program for each of their immersion schools, bearing in mind the academic ability and socio-economic background of the students. We then examined the results for French immersion students on previous assessments of English reading (Jeroski, 1984), mathematics (Robitaille & O'Shea, 1985), and science (Bateson *et al.*, 1986) and compared the performance of French immersion students with that of the comparison students. A more detailed account of the methodology and analyses for this portion of the assessment is provided in O'Shea (1991).

The performance of French immersion students on domain-referenced curriculum tests of English reading, mathematics and science was higher than the average performance of the population of students from districts with immersion programs. Furthermore, French immersion students performed better than students in samples specifically chosen to control for general academic and socio-economic background differences. Many factors, or combinations of factors, may account for the consistently high achievement of French immersion students; these include parental support and encouragement for their children's education; ability and motivational levels of French immersion students; and programmatic effects or instructional practices within the immersion program itself. Regardless of the underlying reasons for differences in achievement, it is clear from the results that immersion students achieve at least as well as, if not better than, regular English program students on provincial objectives in English reading, mathematics and science.

In discussions of French immersion programs in Ontario, researchers suggested a tendency for some immersion programs to be elitist in their student population (Burns, 1986; Olson & Burns, 1983). Yet research shows that immersion programs, particularly early immersion, are suitable for students from a wide range of ability and socio-economic background (Genesee, 1984, 1985, 1991). It will be important to continue to study the ability and background characteristics of the population of students opting for and remaining in immersion programs to ensure that immersion is accessible to and is genuinely serving a broadly based student population.

Subject Matter Testing in French

Since the time of the above provincial assessment, immersion students in British Columbia went on to participate in annual provincial assessments in the subject areas of social studies, mathematics and science. The practice developed to test immersion students in French, using French translated versions of the corresponding English language measures for each subject area. The change to French came about with the growing confidence in student subject matter achievement in English (see previous section) and with a desire to match the language of testing to the language of instruction.

While much information is available on the subject matter achievement of immersion students when they are tested in English, there is considerably less information on how immersion students perform when they write achievement tests in their second language, French. Researchers in Ottawa studied the effects of language of testing on performance (Morrison & Pawley, 1983). Their sample of grade 9 immersion students did equally well in mathematics whether they were tested in French or English. Grade 10 students, on the other hand, performed less well in history when they were tested in French than when they were tested in English. The researchers conclude that the language of testing affects student performance in a language intensive area such as history, suggesting knowledge of technical vocabulary and reading comprehension difficulties as factors to account for the results.

In studies conducted in the province of Alberta, grades 3 and 6 immersion students performed at a lower level when they wrote science, mathematics and social studies tests in French than when they wrote them in English, indicating that student performance is affected by the language of testing (Alberta Education, 1991, 1992). The Alberta studies also reveal that immersion students writing English forms of the tests achieved average scores that were significantly above the provincial average. The authors conclude that French immersion students as a whole have a good command of subject matter achievement but are not as able to demonstrate their knowledge and skills when they are tested in French as when they are tested in English, and they caution against comparing performances on tests written in different languages (Alberta Education, 1992).

Carey (1991) argues for methods of data analysis which will assist teachers, program planners, and curriculum developers in interpreting student performance. Because testing in French may underestimate students' subject matter knowledge, it is important to ensure that those with knowledge about the curriculum, program and students participate in the difficult and complex task of interpreting results.

The British Columbia assessment of science was conducted with this in mind. We served as members of the Contract Team for the provincial assessment of science, taking particular responsibility for French immersion (Bateson et al., 1992a). The assessment involved all grades 4, 7 and 10 French immersion students in the province who had received their science instruction in French in the 1990–91 school year; over 2300 grade 4 and over 1800 grade 7 students from 30 school districts and over 400 grade 10 students from 16 districts participated.

The provincial assessment model was previously described (Figure 1.1). French immersion educators participated closely in all stages of the provincial assessment process and on all committees, thus ensuring as close a link as possible between the assessment of French immersion and regular English program students. The following two additional committees were formed to tailor this assessment to the immersion program's needs: a Translation Review Committee to review the French translations of test items and ensure their appropriateness for immersion students with respect to content and level of language, and a French Interpretation Panel to evaluate the achievement results for French immersion students (see Figure 1.1 (f) and (g)).

Because this was the first time that French immersion students had completed the science assessment in French, there was little information available to assist in interpreting the findings. It was not appropriate to statistically compare French immersion and English program results because the language of testing and the composition of the two groups differed. In visually comparing the performance of the two groups, however, we observed that the mean scores of French immersion students (tested in French) were somewhat lower than those of their English program counterparts (tested in English) in grades 4 and 7 but somewhat higher in grade 10.[2] The results were true for all three goals of the achievement measures (i.e. processes of science, scientific knowledge, and higher level thinking). This pattern of performance was also noted in the British Columbia assessment of social studies in which immersion students had also been tested in French (Cassidy & Bognar, 1991). The results for the elementary grade levels (i.e. grades 4 and 7) were not a cause for concern given previously summarized research indicating that immersion students show high levels of performance in subject matter achievement when tested in English and that testing in French may underestimate their subject matter knowledge.

In order to explore the question further, we examined the individual items on the achievement measures and identified items in which p-values for French immersion and regular English program students differed by ten percentage points or more. Grades 4 and 7 French immersion students differed from English program students by ten percentage points or more on approximately one-third of the items on the achievement measures (34%, 41/120 and 35%, 42/120, respectively).[3] As Table 1.1 indicates, the Interpretation Panel gave linguistic factors as the most frequent reason for the differences in performance in both grades 4 and 7. The panel felt that differences between the two test versions and programmatic or instructional factors accounted for the differences on most of the remaining items.

Table 1.1 Analysis of reasons given by French Interpretation Panel for differences in performance between French immersion and English program students

	Grade 4		Grade 7	
	No. of items	%	No. of items	%
Differences between the two test versions	6	14	3	7
Programmatic/instructional differences	6	14	11	25
Linguistic: vocabulary, formal language structure	29	66	29	66
No reason	3	7	1	2
Total	44[a]		44[b]	

a   Because of cross-categorization, this number is greater than the number of items, which was 41. Grade 4 immersion students' performance was lower than that of English program students on 34 items and higher on 7 items.

b   Because of cross-categorization, this number is greater than the number of items, which was 42. Grade 7 immersion students' performance was lower than that of English program students on 37 items and higher on 5 items.

Among linguistic factors, difficulties with vocabulary were most frequently given as the reason for differences in performance between French and English students. These difficulties posed some interesting problems in testing, which teachers in the Translation Review Committees had not foreseen. Some of the items tested scientific understanding in everyday situations which were familiar to students. A grade 4 item asking students what they should do first if a piece of bread were caught in a toaster illustrates problems in using translated items for different groups of students. The English version of this item contains words that are familiar to English-speaking children (e.g. *toaster, plug, poke*); however, the corresponding words in French may not necessarily be known by immersion students because their experiences in French tend to be limited to the classroom. Even though the translation is correct, the items are not equally difficult in the two languages because of the different linguistic experiences of the two groups.

The Interpretation Panel looked beyond linguistic factors and weighed these with their experience and knowledge of the curriculum and students, and their expectations of performance, in interpreting results and making judgements on student performance. For example, the panel felt that linguistic difficulties on many items in life and physical knowledge also reflected curricular and instructional gaps, and they made recommendations accordingly. There were instances in which panel members maintained their expectations even though they recognized that linguistic difficulties on some items may have lowered performance. For example, in examining grade 7 students' performance on the factual knowledge-life objective, the panel felt that the performance of immersion students could have been better despite difficult vocabulary on some items, and they rated immersion students' performance as 'marginal'; this is in contrast to the Interpretation Panel's judgement of 'satisfactory' for the English program results.

Finally, the panel identified programmatic or instructional factors which contributed to differences in performance, especially on those items where immersion students' performance was higher. Both in grades 4 and 7, these factors included more systematic teaching of metrics in immersion, widespread teaching of the solar system, and emphasis placed on encouraging immersion students to use graphics as a reading strategy.

Overall, French immersion students showed similar areas of strength and weakness in science as students in the regular English program. The French Immersion Interpretation Panel was pleased that students were able to meet the challenge of completing the assessment instruments in their second language, French. In addition to making recommendations for curriculum, instruction and in-service, teachers made recommendations which they felt would help students better access their knowledge in future testing; these included use of visual cues and glossaries for obscure or technical vocabulary, reduction in length of passages and number of questions in French assessments, and separate items for testing more complex skills in the early grades.

It is important to continue the practice of assessing immersion students in the language in which they receive their instruction. The assessment model which involves French immersion teachers as integral members of provincial assessment committees and panels can enhance close collaboration between the two programs and provide worthwhile in-service opportunities for French immersion teachers. Providing immersion teachers with the opportunity to meet separately to consider the results for French immersion can yield valuable programmatic and pedagogical information and increase understanding of students' ability to deal with decontextualized language and complete assessment items in French.

Closing Comments

We have provided a narrative account of our experiences developing a systematic approach to the evaluation of immersion programs, first documenting initial studies commissioned by individual school districts and then more extensive provincial assessments. We have traced the evolution of our work in developing methods to assess difficult to measure areas such as oral proficiency and to design room for the needs of immersion to interface with a large-scale assessment model for the mainstream English program. This provided the base for our research to focus on areas important for the successful implementation of immersion programs, namely, curriculum/instruction and teacher education, the main themes for the next two sections of this book.

Notes

1. Two models of French immersion are currently being offered in British Columbia: early immersion and late immersion. In the early immersion program, all instruction is generally given in French from kindergarten through grade 2. English language arts are introduced in grade 3; and in the intermediate grades (i.e. grades 4–7), other subjects, such as science and mathematics, are also taught in English. In the late immersion program, which begins in grade 6, 80–100% of the instructional time is devoted to French in grades 6 and 7. In secondary school (grades 8–12), early and late immersion students are offered

a follow-up program (secondary immersion), in which French is the language of instruction for approximately 40–60% of the instructional time.

2. The ability of the grade 10 students to close the gap in performance vis-à-vis regular program students shown in the earlier grades may be reflective of the length of time it takes for students to fully develop their academic skills in their second language. Cummins (1981), for example, found that while English second language students develop oral proficiency or communicative skills relatively quickly, they take much longer to develop full academic skills in their second language. Other factors could also contribute to the performance of the grade 10 students. Most immersion students taking science in French in grade 10 have had a sequential program of French science instruction since grade 8, and school districts tend to offer science in French in the secondary grades only if qualified immersion science teachers are available. Attrition in secondary immersion programs (Halsall, 1994; Lewis & Shapson, 1989) may leave a more restricted population as students move through the grades. Students' responses to background questions about their future intentions suggest this: over two-thirds (71.5%) of the grade 10 immersion students said that they planned to take four or more years of further education after secondary school.

3. A full analysis was not completed for grade 10 because there was only a small percentage of items (9%,11/120) where there were program differences.

2 Teaching Grammar in French Immersion: An Experimental Study[1]

Introduction

The results of the evaluation of French speaking in Chapter 1 showed that immersion students were able to engage in fairly complex discussions requiring them to use French for a range of purposes, and that except for fluency they were comparable to native French-speaking students on more communicative measures of speaking (e.g. quality of information, quality of description). The diagnostic information provided through error analyses revealed that students still had major gaps relative to their francophone counterparts in many areas of grammar. Other Canadian research studies reveal a similar pattern of strengths and weaknesses in students' French language performance (e.g. Adiv, 1980, 1984; Day & Shapson, 1987; Harley & Swain, 1984; Lyster, 1987; Swain & Lapkin, 1986). As a result, immersion educators identify improving students' written and oral grammar as a priority in program development and call for curriculum-based research to determine how best to accomplish this. In this chapter, we provide an account of an experimental study conducted in response to this need and designed to investigate whether immersion students' acquisition and use of one specific area of grammar, the conditional, could be improved.

In cooperation with immersion teachers, we developed curricular materials focusing on the conditional and integrating formal, analytic with functional, communicative approaches to language teaching. We designed the materials to teach the conditional by providing opportunities for students to use this form in communicative situations, reinforcing their learning with systematic, focused games or exercises, and encouraging their metalinguistic awareness. The materials were prepared to encourage integration of concepts learned in other subjects (i.e. science and social studies) with language learning and to promote group work and social learning. These instructional features are supported by the research literature on cooperative learning and group work (Kagan, 1986; Long & Porter, 1985); content-based language instruction (Cantoni-Harvey, 1987; Chamot & O'Malley, 1987); metalinguistic awareness (Rutherford, 1987; Sharwood Smith, 1981); and the role of practice in second language learning (McLaughlin, 1990). Thus the implications of this study go beyond immersion to include other kinds of second language teaching situations.

We conducted the experimental study, designed to evaluate the impact of the materials on French language proficiency, in early 1989 in four school districts in the metropolitan area of Vancouver, British Columbia. We exposed an experimental group, composed of six grade 7 early French immersion classes, to the materials over a period of approximately six weeks; and we compared their performance on pre- and posttests of oral and written French with that of a control group, composed of six classes of appropriately matched grade 7 early immersion students, who did not receive the instructional treatment. We also compared their performance on the same measures on follow-up tests administered toward the end of the school year to determine the long-term effects of the treatment.

We chose the conditional as the focus of investigation because research indicated that immersion students make slow progress in gaining productive control over this form in speaking. Harley & Swain (1984) reported accuracy rates of only 15%, 41% and 56% for Ontario immersion students in grades 4, 6 and 10, respectively, compared to an accuracy rate of over 94% for native French-speaking students. In our provincial assessment of immersion (Chapter 1), we found an accuracy rate of 59% for grade 7 early immersion students, compared with 85% for native French-speaking students. Previous research also suggested that students may not receive sufficient exposure to this form in the classroom. Swain & Lapkin (1986) reported that less than 4% of finite verbs used by grades 3 and 6 immersion teachers were in the conditional. Curricular intervention may help overcome this restricted exposure. It may at the same time help promote opportunities for children to use language to express higher level functions (e.g. predicting and hypothesizing), a need identified for both first and second language classrooms (e.g. Chamot & O'Malley, 1987; Shafer et al., 1983; Staab, 1983).

Literature Review

The need to improve immersion children's oral and written grammar is a common concern in Canadian immersion programs. To deal with this, researchers suggest increasing students' opportunities to interact in French in a wider variety of contexts and introducing pedagogical measures in language and subject matter classrooms to enhance students' learning (e.g. Harley, 1993; Lapkin & Swain, 1984; Lentz *et al.*, 1994; Snow *et al.*, 1989). Experimental research based on second language curriculum theory is critically needed to guide and stimulate a systematic approach to curriculum development for language teaching in immersion programs.

Curriculum theorists in second language learning have developed a useful framework for conducting this research. For example, Stern (1982, 1992) proposes a curriculum model requiring the integration of four distinct syllabi – language, culture, communicative activities, and general language education. The language syllabus represents the analytic approach to language study, while the communicative activities allow for experiential use of the language. Allen (1983) argues that there is a need for a three-level framework for curriculum design to bridge the gap between the dichotomous view of second language teaching methods as either manipulation of formal patterns or the full communicative use of language. He advocates a 'variable focus' curriculum model that has the following three components: a structural-analytic component that focuses on grammar and employs controlled grammatical teaching techniques; a functional-analytic component that focuses on discourse features of language and employs controlled communicative teaching techniques; and a non-analytic component that focuses on the natural unanalyzed use of language and employs fully communicative, experiential teaching techniques. These three components are meant to be complementary and would receive varying emphases according to the particular needs and circumstances of the program.

Harley & Swain (1984) suggest that a multi-level model of language teaching such as that proposed by Allen should be investigated for its applicability to immersion, a program mainly based upon the functional, communicative approach. They hypothesize that the immersion approach can be improved by increasing students' exposure to language that is specifically designed to focus their attention on problematic grammatical forms (focused input) and by simultaneously providing students with more opportunities to use the relevant forms in meaningful situations (productive output). Harley (1987a, b, 1989) conducted an experimental study to test this hypothesis, using curricular materials designed to provide focused teaching on the semantic distinctions between the present perfect and the imperfect in combination with extended opportunities for students to use these tenses in meaningful situations. She found that whereas experimental classes were significantly superior to control classes on measures of oral and written French in the short term (i.e. from pre- to posttesting), there were no significant differences over the long term (i.e. both groups improved over time).

We continued the line of investigation initiated by Harley through the study on the conditional presented in this chapter. Our study is similar to Harley's in design and in many procedures; however, it focuses on a different point of grammar and uses a slightly older age group of students (grade 7 versus grade 6). The experimental materials we developed also differ from those by Harley in that they require more instructional time and incorporate various instructional features (e.g. cooperative learning approach and group evaluation procedures) designed to maximize student interaction and encourage conscious awareness of language use. Subsequent to our study, Lyster (1994a) also conducted an experimental study in the line initiated by Harley. His study focused on sociolinguistic variation in the use of *tu* and *vous*, involved grade 8 immersion students, and used materials with a stronger analytic focus than did either our or Harley's study.

It is important to point out that the overall approach to language teaching in these studies diverges from Krashen's widely discussed theory on second language learning, which ascribes only limited importance to production and grammatical teaching in fostering second language acquisition. According to Krashen (1981, 1984), comprehensible input is the only causative variable in second language acquisition; production is not a cause but rather a result of acquisition and therefore plays only a limited role in promoting acquisition. Grammatical teaching is largely ineffective in promoting subconscious acquisition, which is the major determinant of fluency in a language. Such teaching can only contribute to conscious learning, which can be used as a monitor to edit or correct speech only under certain conditions. Swain (1985) challenges Krashen's position, arguing that production has an important function in forcing the language learner to move from meaning to grammar. According to this view, 'producing the target language acts as one of the triggers that force language learners to pay attention to the means of expression needed to successfully convey their intended meaning' (Swain & Lapkin, 1986: 7). Although we cannot isolate the effects of a single variable on second language learning in this experimental study, we hope that we can provide information relevant to the theoretical debate on the importance of production and grammatical teaching in the language acquisition process. We also hope to lend support to recent classroom-based research investigating the role of instruction in communicative language learning situations (e.g. Lightbown & Spada, 1990; Spada & Lightbown, 1993; White, 1991).

Methodology

Sample

The sample consisted of 315 grade 7 early immersion students from four school districts in the metropolitan Vancouver area. In all, 12 classes participated in the study, with two classes each from two districts and four classes each from the remaining two districts. We selected the participating classes with the help of district administrative personnel, who were asked to recommend grade 7 immersion classes that were most similar to one another in general socio-economic background and ability levels of the students and teaching experience of the teachers. Split classes were excluded. We had a limited pool from which to make the selection in each district, with two of three or four eligible classes chosen in two districts (Districts A and B), and all four or four of five eligible classes chosen in the other two districts (Districts C and D).

We stratified assignment of classes to experimental or control groups by district and assigned classes on a random basis, using the pretest results and the information provided by the school districts to match the two groups. In all, there were six classes in both the experimental group and the control group. The number of students in each class ranged from 23 to 30 students in the experimental group and from 24 to 29 in the control group. Table 2.1 summarizes the distribution of the student sample.

Table 2.1 Distribution of student sample (n = 315)

School district	Experimental group School[a]	Class	n	Control group School[a]	Class	n
A	1	1	23	1	1	29
B	1	1	23	1	1	26
C	2	2	26/27	2	2	28/28
D	1	2[b]	27/30	1	2[b]	24/24
Total	5	6	156	5	6	159

a Except for the all-immersion schools in District D, all schools are dual-track schools (i.e. schools in which both a regular English program and a French immersion program are operating).
b One teacher taught the French immersion component to both classes.

The total number of teachers involved was five in each of the experimental and control groups. We asked teachers to complete a questionnaire designed to gather information to judge the comparability of the experimental and control classes. The questionnaire information indicated that both the experimental and the control teachers had an average of 5.4 years, teaching experience. Except for one experimental and one control teacher who indicated that they were 'anglophone with a good mastery of French', all teachers described themselves as being either 'totally bilingual with equal competence in French and English' or 'francophone with a good mastery of English'.

The average amount of instructional time in French was approximately three hours a day for both the experimental and control classes. Except for one teacher who said that his/her class was 'above average', all experimental teachers indicated that their grade 7 immersion class was 'average' in French language ability. There was more variability in the responses of the control teachers: one control teacher indicated an 'average' class; one, an 'above average' class; and one, a class in between these two categories; the remaining two teachers indicated classes of 'mixed ability'.

Design and analyses

This study had an experimental design, with an experimental group composed of six grade 7 early French immersion classes from four school districts and a control group composed of six classes of appropriately matched grade 7 early French immersion students from the same school districts. The experimental group received the treatment, which was a specifically designed curriculum unit focusing on the conditional, over the period of 5 to 7 weeks. The control group received their normal classroom instruction. We administered written and oral measures of French to both groups prior to the onset of the experimental treatment (pretest) and immediately after its completion (posttest). We administered tests toward the end of the school year to determine the long-term effects of the treatment (follow-up test).

We conducted statistical comparisons between the pretest results of the experimental and control groups to determine their relative standing at the start of the experiment. Repeated measures analysis of variance was used to statistically compare the growth of the two groups in French writing and speaking over the three testing times (i.e. pre, post, and follow-up). Only students who had participated at all three testing sessions were included. We combined the data for the two forms of each test for the analyses, as acceptable correlations had been obtained between the pilot version forms

(Pearson Correlation Coefficient, 0.76 for the cloze test and 0.73 for the written composition).

Procedures

Following pretesting of all classes in early January, we assigned classes to experimental or control groups on a stratified random basis and sent the teachers of the experimental classes an information letter explaining the design and purpose of the project and notifying them of their participation. We also sent the experimental teachers a copy of the curriculum unit and asked that they review it in preparation for a training workshop held near the end of January. All experimental teachers attended the workshop, which provided information on the rationale of the project, the experimental materials, and the conduct of the experiment. Teachers were asked to teach the curriculum unit over a 5–6 week period beginning in the first week of February. We made classroom observations at different times during the experimental period to gain familiarity with the use of the materials in a classroom situation.

The curriculum unit was designed to be used within a 5–6 week period. However, because of various other classroom activities and projects, it took longer for some experimental classes to complete the unit and thus, the length of the experimental period varied from five to seven weeks. We scheduled the posttesting in March to accommodate this variation. Experimental classes were tested during the week immediately following the completion of the unit, and control classes were tested during the same week as were the corresponding experimental classes in their district. We scheduled the follow-up testing so that classes would be tested 11 weeks following the time of their posttesting (late May, early June).

Description of experimental materials

The experimental materials consist of a curriculum unit focusing on the use of the conditional in hypothetical situations and in polite requests and involve students in planning an imaginary space colony. We designed the materials, which have a primarily functional-analytic focus in terms of Allen's model, to capitalize on the highly developed proficiency skills of immersion students and to mirror the conditions found to be of critical importance in effective second language learning programs. Genesee (1987) identifies these as integration of second language teaching and content teaching; classroom interaction characterized by negotiation of meaning; and a curriculum of study that is intrinsically motivating.

Some of the major instructional features include the use of: (a) the cooperative learning approach to maximize student interaction and use of the conditional in communicative situations; (b) linguistic games and exercises regularly preceding or initiating each period to reinforce the use of this form in more formal, structured situations; (c) a thematic, task-based approach to provide a substantive basis for language learning; and (d) group- and self-evaluation procedures to encourage students to develop conscious awareness of their language use, particularly with respect to the conditional. In these procedures, one student is designated to be the 'monitor of French' during each meeting and is asked to record each time the conditional is used and each time English is spoken on evaluation forms provided in the student folders.

The curriculum unit includes the following major group activities: planning of a space colony; presentation of an oral report describing and justifying the students' plan; making a model of the plan; preparation of a written report describing each part of the colony and its importance; and preparation of a newspaper article describing the life of the space pioneers. The unit is designed to be used over a period of 5–6 weeks, with approximately three 45–60-minute periods per week. A package of supplementary materials containing suggestions for follow-up is provided for teachers to use on an optional basis after the experiment. An outline of the curriculum unit and a description of the linguistic games are presented in Table 2.2 and Figure 2.1.

All materials required for teaching the unit were provided to the teachers in the experimental group. These were written in French and included: a teacher's guide, a series of envelopes containing the student materials, a classroom poster explaining the organization of student groups, and student folders for keeping materials. Two introductory sections provided an overview of the unit, a descriptive summary of the various uses of the conditional, and the procedures for forming student groups and evaluating group work. Subsequent sections outlined the goals and objectives and the procedures for conducting the major activities and provided detailed instructions, suggested timelines, and student materials for all tasks. A teacher questionnaire was placed at the end of each task and at the end of the curriculum unit. The questionnaires, which were adapted from those developed by Harley (1989), were designed to provide information on how much time teachers spent and to gain their opinions on student interest in the various tasks and the unit as a whole, as well as their appropriateness and effectiveness. Teachers were asked to mail all completed questionnaires to our research team after they had completed the unit.

Table 2.2 Curriculum unit: outline of activities

Strategy	Task	Description
Introduction and Activity 1		
(Approximately nine 45-minute periods)		
Teacher		Formation of groups; Linguistic Game A
Group work	I	Planning a space colony: discussion of elements essential for human survival and preliminary plan[a]
	II	Discussion of futuristic elements in *Surréal 3000* (Chapters 1–3)[a]
Individual work		Self-evaluation
Group work	III	Preparation of oral report[a]
Group work	IV	Presentation and evaluation of oral reports[a]
Group work	V	Revision of the plan[a]
Individual work		Self-evaluation
Activity 2		
(Approximately six 45-minute periods)		
Group work	I	Making a drawing, model, or collage of the plan[a]
Group work	II	Selection of ten most important elements in the space colony and preparation of a written report explaining their function[a]
Group work	III	Preparation of a newspaper article describing the life of the space pioneers[a]
Individual work		Self-evaluation

a Each period is preceded by a linguistic game or warm-up exercise based on the games.

Various student materials were provided, including information about the theme of the unit, instructions for the tasks and linguistic games, glossaries of linguistic expressions, and group and self-evaluation sheets. The conditional was used wherever possible in the text to provide students with exposure to printed material containing this form. The materials were distributed to the students by the teachers as they were needed. Students were required to keep all materials related to the project, along with their written work, in folders provided with the curriculum unit.

Linguistic Game A, *Le conditionnel et la politesse*

The teacher first explains the use of the conditional for making polite requests and provides the rules for forming the conditional. Student groups are given ten sentences and are asked to rephrase the sentences to make them more polite. They are then asked to create and role-play situations in which requests are made first by an authoritarian and then by a courteous person.

Linguistic Game B, *Jeu des hypothèses*

This game is designed to encourage students to use the conditional in hypothetical situations. Students are provided with eight scientific situations in which they are asked to discuss what would happen if certain specified changes were made in each of them.

Linguistic Game C, *Jeu des Si . . ., alors*

Version 1. The teacher writes on the board a list of hypothetical clauses beginning with *Si . . ., alors* and gives student groups ten minutes to make up as many endings as possible. The teacher then chooses one of the hypothetical clauses at random and asks one of the groups to complete it in as many ways as possible in 30 seconds. The teacher then continues with the remaining clauses and groups. One point is assigned each time a correct conditional is used, and the group with the greatest number of points is named the winner.

Version 2. This version is similar to Version 1 except that students work with a different set of hypothetical clauses and individually prepare written responses at home. The individual responses are reviewed in each group before playing the game, as outlined in Version 1.

Version 3. Student groups make up their own hypothetical clauses and ask the other groups to complete them.

Version 4. A list of 20 hypothetical clauses is distributed to all students, and they are asked to write an ending to each of these.

Version 5. Students make up their own hypothetical sentences, using the first and second persons singular or plural.

Figure 2.1 Description of linguistic games

Instruments

The instruments developed for the study consist of a cloze test, a written composition, and an oral interview. There were two forms for each of the three tests. We distributed these randomly in the pretesting so that half the students in each class received Form A and the other half received Form B. We reversed this distribution in the posttesting so that students received a different form than they had in the pretesting; we maintained the original distribution in the follow-up so that students received the same form as in the pretest. All students in the class received the composition and the cloze test, in that order; and a sample of nearly one-third of the students (eight students per class), randomly selected by the examiner at the time of pretesting, received the oral interview.

Three trained francophone examiners conducted all testing following standardized procedures we had developed. Students wrote the composition and cloze tests in their own classrooms, and they were interviewed on a different day in a quiet room, separate from the classroom. The interviews were recorded. A description of the instruments and the scoring procedures follows.

Cloze tests

These tests consisted of French dialogues in which blanks were substituted for missing verbs. Students were asked to complete the dialogue by putting the verbs, which were provided in infinitive form under the blanks, in the correct tense. There were 32 blanks in each form; of these, 27 were required to be in the conditional, and the remaining in present or past tenses. Only the conditional verbs were scored, using the rules described below for the written composition. Test reliabilities for this test were established on the basis of the pretest results ($\alpha = 0.92$).

Written compositions

Students were instructed to choose a comic character (Form A) or a famous person (Form B) that they would like to be and to write a paragraph beginning with the words *Si j' étais* . . . .. They were given a maximum of 15 minutes to complete this task. The paragraphs were scored by determining the number of obligatory conditional contexts supplied by the student and by examining the verbs in these contexts. If a verb was not in the conditional, it was scored as 0; if a verb was in the conditional, it was scored as 1, 2 or 3 according to the degree of correctness of the forms. A mean score was calculated based on the ratio of total number of points received to the total number of conditional contexts multiplied by three.

Oral interviews

We designed the oral interviews to elicit the use of the conditional in hypothetical situations. One question was also included to elicit the conditional of politeness. Both forms contained a preliminary warm-up section that included questions on the student's age, family and previous or forthcoming vacation. In Form A, students were shown a Club Med Album to browse through and were then asked to talk about where they would go and what they would do if they won a two-week holiday. After talking freely on their ideal holiday, they were asked what they would do in the evening, what their parents would do, and what they would do if they were given $500 spending money. In the second part of the interview, students were requested to play the role of an interviewer and to ask the examiner questions about an ideal holiday. To elicit the conditional of politeness, they were told first to ask the examiner for the microphone. If they did not use the conditional, they were asked to rephrase their request in a more polite fashion. Form B followed a similar format as did Form A, except that students were shown an album of Vancouver and were asked to talk about what they would do if they were to spend three days in Vancouver with a few young visitors from out of town.

Students' voices were recorded. All tapes were transcribed in an orthographic transcription complemented by a phonetic transcription where necessary. All obligatory contexts for the conditional were calculated, and verbs used in these contexts were scored. The scoring procedures were similar to those developed for the written tests except that Category 2, which is applicable only to written language, was not used.

A native French-speaking marker, who was trained using the pilot-test samples, completed the scoring of the written tests immediately after each testing session. We made frequent calibration checks with the marker and determined inter-rater reliabilities (between marker and researcher) on a randomly chosen set of the pre- and posttests. The results revealed that inter-rater reliabilities were quite high in all cases (Pearson Correlation Coefficient, 0.978 and higher). To control for scoring reliability over the three scoring times, the marker was asked to rescore a randomly chosen set of each of the pretest instruments with the posttests and a randomly chosen set of posttest instruments with the follow-up tests. The results revealed high intra-rater reliabilities over the three sessions (0.993 and higher). The oral interview samples were scored after the three testing sessions were completed. They were scored twice by the native French-speaking marker with our collaboration.

Results

Statistical analyses of group results

Pretest

Preliminary analyses comparing the performance of the experimental and control groups at the time of pretesting indicated that there were no significant differences between the two groups on either the written or the oral measures (see Table 2.3).

Table 2.3 Pretest: results of statistical comparisons between the scores of the experimental and control groups

	Experimental group			Control group			
	n	$\overline{X}$	SD	n	$\overline{X}$	S.D	t-value
Cloze test	149	16.6	14.2	153	18.3	17.0	0.93*
Written composition	147	44.0	26.6	152	45.8	29.0	0.55*
Oral interview	48	31.6	22.7	47	35.3	22.3	0.81*

* = not significant

Experimental effects

The results of the repeated measures analysis of variance using the class as the unit of analysis (see Table 2.4) revealed that there was a significant group-by-time interaction on the cloze test and written composition, with the experimental group making greater gains than did the control group on these measures. There was no significant group-by-time interaction on the oral interview. The ANOVA results using the student as the unit of analysis revealed a similar pattern, with a significant group-by-time interaction on the written measures but not on the oral measure.

The results of post hoc comparisons (Tukey's HSD) indicated that the experimental group performed significantly higher than did the control group on the cloze test and written composition both in the posttesting (HSD = 8.71† and 7.71†, respectively) and in the follow-up testing eleven weeks later (HSD = 7.77† and 10.60†, respectively).

Figure 2.2 contains a graphic presentation of the group means for the three testing sessions (i.e. pre, post, and follow-up). Both the experimental and the control groups improved their performance on the written and oral measures from pre- to posttesting, and they maintained this improved performance in the follow-up testing (except for a slight decline for the control group on the written composition). The experimental group,

Table 2.4 Results of repeated measures analysis of variance (class as unit of analysis)

Source	df	Mean squares	F-ratio
Cloze test			
Group	1	510.609	1.51*
Time	2	1173.211	26.79‡
Group × time	2	196.781	4.49**
Within subjects	20	43.794	
Written composition			
Group	1	1010.531	2.94*
Time	2	1328.906	19.86‡
Group × time	2	361.477	5.40†
Within subjects	20	66.903	
Oral interview			
Group	1	81.680	0.25*
Time	2	1673.461	27.13‡
Group × time	2	114.773	1.86*
Within subjects	20	61.681	

* = not significant, ** = significant at the 0.020 level, † = significant at the 0.010 level, ‡ = significant at the 0.001 level.

however, made more improvement than the control group, with pretest to follow-up gains ranging from 11 to 21 points higher than those of the control group over this period.

Descriptive analyses of class results

We examined the results for the individual classes in order to determine whether there were any differences in the pattern of growth among classes in either the experimental or the control group. Almost all experimental and control classes improved their performance on the oral and written measures from pre- to posttesting (see Figures 2.3–2.5). However, the growth of the experimental classes is more consistent from class to class, whereas the growth of the control classes is uneven. One control class (Class I), in particular, accounted for most of the gains made by the control classes on the written measures, and the same class, along with one other class (Class J), accounted for most of the gains on the oral measure.

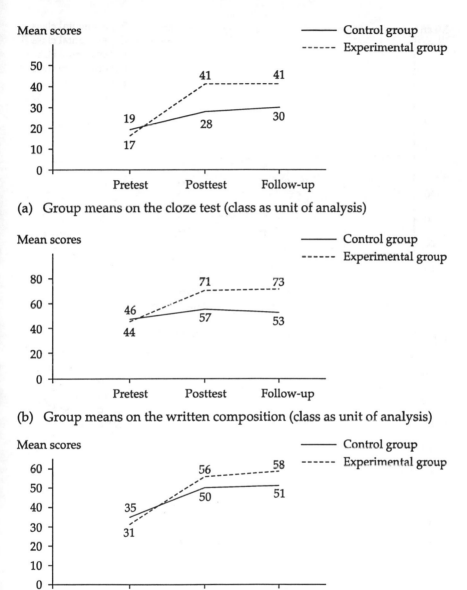

(a) Group means on the cloze test (class as unit of analysis)

(b) Group means on the written composition (class as unit of analysis)

(c) Group means on the oral interview (class as unit of analysis)

Figure 2.2 Group mean scores

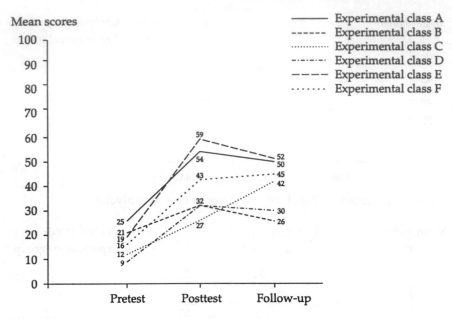

(a) Experimental group class means on cloze test

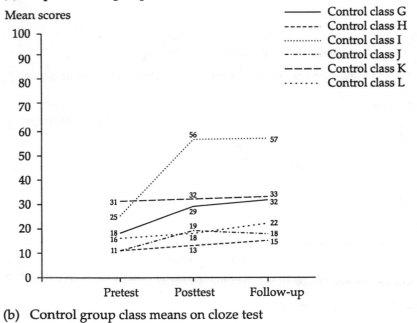

(b) Control group class means on cloze test

Figure 2.3 Class means on cloze test

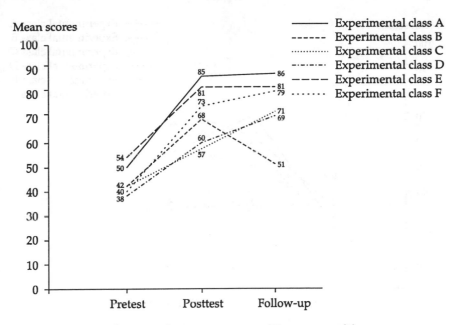

(a) Experimental group class means on written composition

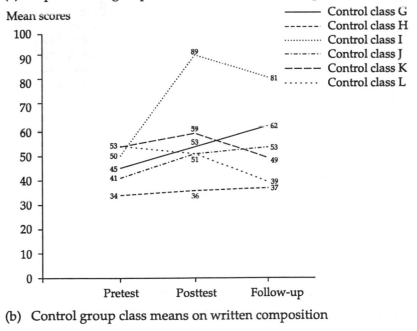

(b) Control group class means on written composition

Figure 2.4 Class means on written composition

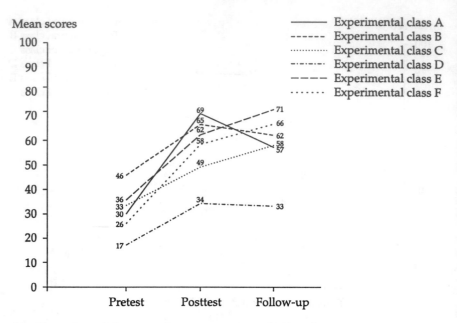

(a) Experimental group class means on oral interview

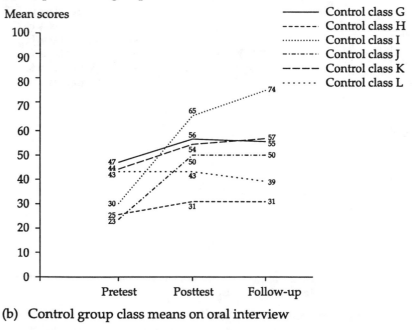

(b) Control group class means on oral interview

Figure 2.5 Class means on oral interview

Information obtained from a questionnaire sent to the experimental and control teachers to gather background and descriptive information is helpful in interpreting the performance of this class (Class I). The teacher of this class reported that over half of the students (16/29) had been classified as 'gifted'. This teacher, who had previously taught in the Federal Government's language training program, indicated that he had taught all verb tenses since January, with 5–10 hours spent on the conditional versus 3–4 hours or less reported by the teachers of the other control classes. The teacher said that he combined grammatical teaching with practice through oral activities and written tasks and generally placed a great deal of emphasis on oral activities in teaching. Although cooperative learning was not used to any great extent, overall the information provided suggests that this control teacher's instructional methods resembled those in the experimental curriculum unit in that grammar was taught through a combination of formal and functional approaches and a great deal of emphasis was placed on oral and written activities.

Teacher information and opinions on the curriculum unit

The average number of hours teachers said it had taken them to complete the unit was 17.4, with one teacher specifying 17 hours, two specifying 15 hours, and two specifying 20 hours. The mean rating for the question asking teachers how much they thought their students enjoyed the various activities in the curriculum unit was 3.8 (max. = 5), indicating that overall students 'much' enjoyed the activities. The mean rating for the question asking teachers to evaluate the level of difficulty of the unit was 3.2 (max. = 5), indicating an overall 'average' level of difficulty; and the mean rating for the question asking teachers whether they thought the educational objectives of the unit had been attained was 3.8, indicating that overall teachers felt that the educational objectives had been 'well' attained. Teachers' open-ended comments at the end of the questionnaire were also very positive and revealed considerable enthusiasm and support for the experimental materials. Information from the questionnaire sent to all teachers at the end of the school year indicated that only one teacher used the supplementary activities provided as a follow-up to the unit. However, most teachers said that they tried to reinforce the use of the conditional in various ways.

Summary and Conclusions

In their research agenda for immersion programs, Lapkin *et al.* (1990) identify how best to integrate grammar teaching into French immersion as a key question for investigation. We designed this experimental study to address this question. We found that classes that had experienced an approach which integrated formal, analytic and functional, communicative activities in teaching the conditional made significantly higher gains in their ability to use this form in writing than did classes which had not experienced this approach. Statistically significant gains were not revealed in speaking. However, when we examined the individual class data, we found greater and more consistent growth in speaking for the experimental than for the control classes, suggesting that they benefited somewhat from the experimental treatment in this domain as well.

The relatively smaller gains made by students in speaking than in writing may be attributed to several factors. Among these are the commonly observed lag between assimilation of a new rule and its automatization in speaking, as well as the competition provided by previously automatized rules in the learner's grammar (James, 1980; McLaughlin, 1990). In the detailed error analyses of the speaking data, we noted the presence of interlanguage forms (e.g. use of infinitive, periphrastic future, *vouloir* and infinitive and the adverb *peut-être* to express the hypothetical notion) similar to those found in studies of younger immersion children (Harley & Swain, 1977). In addition, in the classroom observations we conducted during the experiment, we noted more variation among groups in the extent to which they used the conditional in speaking, when discussion was open-ended and the product transitory, than in writing, when there was a visible product that could be edited and corrected. Although we feel that the inclusion of a 'French language monitor' was helpful as a technique for promoting grammatical consciousness in an overall sense, it may not have been completely successful in encouraging groups to use the conditional consistently in the freer speaking tasks when children were more interested in the meaning of the message they wanted to convey than in its form. Finally, in some speaking tasks, we noticed a tendency for students to contextualize their speech in the present, thus eliminating the need to use the conditional, which expresses hypothetical meaning in the past.

When we considered the individual class data in this study, we found that one control class in particular was responsible for most of the growth made by the control classes on the writing and speaking measures. Information gained from the teacher of this class provided some clues as to why this was the case. These included an unusually high percentage of 'gifted' students in the class, a greater amount of time spent teaching the conditional than was spent in other control classes (i.e. 5–10 hours versus 3–4 hours or less), and the teacher's instructional approach which resembled the approach used in the experimental materials. Under these circumstances, it should perhaps not be surprising that this strong class showed a growth pattern which was more similar to that displayed by the experimental than by the control classes. These circumstances, however, do not normally occur in the majority of immersion classrooms, and the results reinforce the need for the systematic introduction of curricular materials of the kind used in the present study. As well, there is a critical need for observational research to be conducted in immersion classrooms so that effective strategies currently being used by immersion teachers to promote grammatical growth can be identified.

The findings of our study, and those of Lyster's (1994a) subsequent study on sociolinguistic variation in the use of *tu* and *vous*, differ from the findings of the previously mentioned study by Harley (1989), who found only short-term and no long-term benefits accruing from the introduction of grammatically focused curricular materials in immersion classrooms. However, our study differs from the Harley study in the age group of the subjects (grade 7 versus grade 6) and in the grammatical focus of the experimental materials (conditional vs. present perfect and imperfect). The experimental materials we developed also differ from those developed by Harley in the amount and intensity of instruction (17.4 hours over six weeks versus 11.9 hours over eight weeks) and the use of a thematic, task-based approach, cooperative learning, and group evaluation procedures. Any one or all of these differences may have contributed to the somewhat different pattern of results and deserve consideration in the future design of curricular materials for immersion programs. Also worthy of consideration are factors Lyster (1994a) suggests contributed to the beneficial effects of his treatment; these include the linguistic simplicity of the feature being taught and a stronger analytic focus in the experimental materials, which he suggests was possible because of the older age group of students (i.e. grade 8) involved.

Overall, our study suggests that immersion students' oral and written grammatical skills can be improved through curricular intervention which combines formal, analytic with functional, communicative approaches to language teaching. Especially because of the consistency of the results for experimental classes, we think that this integrated approach holds much promise for improving language learning in immersion programs, particularly in those areas in which the functional richness of grammar can be explored (e.g. the verb system that has been found to be a major area of difficulty for immersion students; see Harley, 1993). The speaking results, however, suggest that more time and effort may be needed to allow students to assimilate fully their new grammatical learning. This is recognized in traditional second language programs by a curriculum in which specific areas of grammar are reintroduced and revisited over a period of years. It would be worthwhile for immersion programs to consider more fully the need for long-term and systematic curriculum planning to ensure the continued progress of students. This is particularly important in view of research showing that the effects of grammatical instruction are not always long-lasting (Lightbown, 1991).

We cannot separate the benefits that may have accrued from the increased opportunities for comprehension provided by the materials in this study from those that may have accrued from the increased opportunities for production. Therefore, we cannot help resolve the theoretical debate on the importance of production in second language learning (cf. Genesee, 1987; Krashen, 1981; Swain, 1985). Nor can we isolate the effects of the various instructional features of the experimental materials, such as the linguistic games, that provided focused input, the cooperative learning approach, that encouraged productive output, and the group and self-evaluation procedures, that encouraged conscious awareness of language use. Whereas this information is important and would contribute to our understanding of both theoretical and practical issues in second language learning, we should not preclude the possibility that the key to improving second language performance in the classroom may lie in the totality of the individual instructional features rather than in their isolation. It may also lie in the more general characteristics of the experimental materials that, in addition to providing a systematic grammatical focus, stimulated metalinguistic awareness and created an interactive and motivating learning environment in which language learning could take place.

Note

1. This chapter is based on the article with a similar title appearing in *Language Learning* (1991) 41, 25–58.

3 Integrating Language and Science in Immersion Classrooms: A Case Study Approach

Introduction

In the 1980s, many researchers became concerned with the overemphasis of research on the outcomes of immersion education and the lack of contextual and process information on how the program might best function instructionally (Calvé, 1988; Carey, 1984; Genesee, 1987; Lapkin *et al.*, 1990; Tardif & Weber, 1987). Since that time, observational studies of immersion classrooms have begun to appear in Canada (Laplante, 1993; Netten & Spain, 1989; Swain & Carroll, 1987; Tardif, 1991, 1994; Weber, 1991; Weber & Tardif, 1991) and internationally (Artigal, 1991; Bernhardt, 1992; Vesterbacka, 1991). However, considerable empirical information is still needed on classroom processes, in particular, how immersion teachers integrate language and subject matter teaching.

> Lacking such information, we are poorly prepared to train teachers
> . . . A program of research to investigate how immersion teachers
> integrate academic and language instruction is called for. (Genesee,
> 1987: 185)

Immersion teachers' beliefs about language and subject matter teaching also help us gain a better understanding of classroom practices (see Laplante, 1996; Salomone, 1992a). This is consistent with recent research on teacher thinking which stresses the importance of exploring teachers' views on learning and instruction as a basis for understanding and improving classroom practices and professional preparation (Breen, 1991; Clark, 1988; Cumming, 1989; Hollingsworth, 1989; Johnson, 1992; Richardson *et al.*, 1991).

41

During the 1990–91 school year, we participated in a provincial study designed to gain knowledge of classroom practices and contexts in which British Columbia students learn about science.[1] The study, henceforth referred to as the Context for Science Study, included 48 regular English and 12 French immersion classes in grades 4, 7 and 10, and involved on-site observations of schools and classrooms and interviews with teachers, students and administrators (Wideen *et al.*, 1992). Information collected for French immersion addressed the following questions:

(1) How do immersion teachers integrate language and science teaching?

(2) What do immersion teachers say about their language and science teaching and various aspects of their language and science pedagogy?

Because of the exploratory nature of the topic and the small sample of immersion classrooms, we used a case study approach to examine these questions so that we could gain 'insights into the phenomenon under study' (Merriam, 1988: 21). In this chapter, we present four case studies, which we have selected from a data set of 12, in order to describe and discuss various aspects of the topic of language and subject matter integration (cf. Agar, 1980). Two cases reflect constrasting approaches to language and science teaching, a third illustrates the dual role the immersion teacher plays in integrating language and science, and a fourth leaves us with interesting questions for continuing inquiry. Although the case studies portray actual classroom events and interview discourse, we have altered details and used fictitional names to maintain anonymity of participants.

Literature Review

A central theoretical concept is the view of language learning as a process of creative construction, in which the child is seen as an independent agent actively constructing meaning, formulating linguistic rules, and organizing the language he/she hears (Dulay *et al.*, 1982). The following are hypothesized to play a key role in second language learning:

- comprehensible input (the amount of language which the learner can fully understand plus a little bit more, which challenge the learner to progress beyond his/her current level; Krashen, 1981);
- negotiation of meaning and social interaction which emphasizes mutuality and reciprocity in the meanings that are constructed and negotiated through talk (Wells, 1981; Wells & Chang-Wells, 1992);
- productive language use which enables learners to test out hypotheses about the language and encourages them to pay attention to the

means of expression needed to successfully convey meaning (Swain, 1985).

Basing her work on current theory and on a survey of immersion teachers in the United States, Snow (1987, 1989) specified core instructional strategies and techniques used by immersion teachers to foster language and subject matter learning in their classrooms. These include explicit teacher modeling of language; extensive use of body language, visuals, and manipulatives; building redundancy into lessons; use of clarification/comprehension checks; encouraging productive use of language; and indirect error correction.

While these strategies are consistent with theoretical perspectives on second language learning, empirical evidence is needed on the manner and extent to which immersion teachers actually incorporate these strategies into their subject matter teaching. Tardif & Weber observed that kindergarten and grade 1 immersion teachers used contextual clues and paralinguistic elements and modified their discourse through self-repetitions, linguistic modeling and paraphrase; these provided 'scaffolds' which enabled children to understand what was required of them and make sense of their learning experiences (Tardif, 1991, 1994; Weber, 1991). Laplante (1993) observed similar strategies in his study of a grade 1 science classroom and described interaction strategies which served to facilitate students' language production and enable them to participate in a variety of language tasks. Salomone's (1992a, b) research in immersion classes in the United States also reveals a rich array of strategies employed by immersion teachers.

Swain & Carroll (1987) found certain limitations in the language learning conditions of the grades 3 and 6 immersion classrooms they observed. Specifically, the researchers found that students had little opportunity to produce sustained discourse in French. Swain & Carroll also found that teachers rarely focused students' attention on the relationship of form to meaning when they taught subject matter and provided unsystematic feedback to students about their linguistic errors. In addition, the language of the classroom was functionally restricted in some ways, with certain uses of the language (e.g. the conditional verb form; aspectual distinctions in verb tenses) occurring infrequently in teachers' speech.

Reflecting on the results of this study, Swain (1987) recommends that immersion teachers introduce activities which allow students both to hear and produce language in its full functional range. She also recommends that they encourage students to become more aware of the relationship between form and meaning as they use the language in their learning and that they develop more systematic and creative strategies for correcting students' errors.

Snow *et al.* (1989) make a more specific proposal for improving the language learning potential of immersion classrooms. In addition to dealing with *content obligatory* language objectives, which specify the language students need to develop, master and communicate about a given content material, immersion teachers are called upon to strengthen the link between language and subject matter teaching by systematically identifying and including *content compatible* linguistic objectives in their teaching. These can derive from analysis of students' language or communication difficulties and be used by teachers to provide for increased exposure to correct structures and extended use through student practice.

The preceding discussion deals largely with the strengthening of content teaching to promote language learning objectives. One possible danger of this perspective, although not at all intended by researchers, is that content or subject matter may be seen only as providing the context for learning language and consequently be deemphasized. In addition, surface features of language may be stressed, and the critical role language plays as a medium for learning in all subject areas may be overlooked. Working in English second language education, Mohan (1986) proposes a theoretical framework which unites language and content by connecting underlying knowledge structures with thinking processes and with language notions or meanings. Because it reflects an inquiry approach to learning and a semantic orientation to language, Mohan's work may help immersion teachers develop a way of thinking about the integration of language and content that could help them go beyond the more surface aspects of linguistic and subject matter mastery.

The importance of 'using language to learn' is also stressed in first language instruction in the language across the curriculum movement (Bullock Committee, 1975; Corson, 1990), whole language and writing process approaches (Altwerger *et al.*, 1987; Graves, 1983), and sociocultural theory (Wells & Chang-Wells, 1992). Lindfors (1980:271) describes a classroom environment where children's language is used most powerfully for learning as one which: (a) fosters children's exploration and active questioning; (b) focuses clearly on children's meaningful communication and problem-solving, with skills development activities supporting this focus; (c) encourages 'languaging' and conceptualizing at the higher levels of cognitive processing rather than at the lower levels; (d) encourages interaction among the children, thus supporting their development toward increased mental flexibility and a more variable point of view; and (e) includes a teacher who is an active, ongoing learner in the classroom community.

The 'using language to learn' perspective is joined by more cognitive views of learning that have recently gained prominence in science and other subject areas. In current perspectives on science teaching, learners are seen as actively constructing meaning, bringing prior beliefs to experiences and gradually modifying their beliefs as they interact with new experiences and the ideas of others (Millar & Driver, 1987; Osborne & Freyberg, 1985). In addition, in contrast with previous views of science as an accumulation of facts, rules, and definitions or a set of process skills, the content of science teaching is being redefined to emphasize the explanatory functions of science, with scientific knowledge viewed as tentative and as our best attempt to explain how and why things happen in the natural world (Anderson, 1987). In Cuevas' (1990) summary of recent work concerned with the teaching and learning of science, he identifies as an important premise the language necessary for children to understand and interpret science content and communicate proficiently in class. He notes the explicit bridge between the teaching of content and the development of language. Perhaps Anderson's description of the science classroom as a 'learning community' can help us visualize the important role of language in science learning:

> Students should be actively engaged not just in learning facts and practicing skills, but in practicing the activities of scientifically literate adults: explanation, description, prediction, and control of objects and events in the natural world. Students in such an ideal learning community learn science from sources of *authority* such as textbooks and the teacher, from *evidence* that they acquire by working with natural objects and events, and from *communication* with each other and their teacher. (Anderson, 1987: 87)

Methodology

The approach to the Context for Science Study is based on educational ethnography (or quasi-ethnography), designed to provide rich, descriptive data about the contexts, activities and beliefs of participants in educational settings (Goetz & LeCompte, 1984). We briefly summarize those aspects of the methodology needed to understand the case studies of immersion classrooms (for further detail, see Wideen *et al.*, 1992; Day, 1993).

Sampling and instruments

The classroom sample included 12 French immersion classrooms, four each at grades 4, 7 and 10. It is important to note that the sample was not large enough nor intended to be a statistical representation; therefore, the results should *not* be used to generalize across districts or classrooms. Data were collected through on-site observations and interviews at the district, school and classroom levels. The case studies are based on two intensive classroom observations per class and teacher interviews, with information gathered in school observations and student interviews used as additional sources of triangulation.

An extensive interview-observation package was developed for the study; this included structured interview protocols for teachers and students. The Teacher Interview Schedule consists of open-ended questions on various topics, including teachers' views on the nature and importance of science; beliefs and rationales for various aspects of teachers' science and language pedagogy; beliefs and practices in integrating subject matter and in integrating language and science; and context for science and French teaching, including school and district policy, procedure and practice. The Student Interview Schedule consists of open-ended questions designed to gain student opinions on the nature and purpose of science, views about scientists, descriptions of and attitudes toward school science, and views about learning, future school science and careers.

Procedures

Research team members spent approximately two days in each school, conducting classroom observations and interviews, observing the school, library, and science equipment room, and talking to school personnel informally in the staffroom. Classroom observations and all except informal interviews in the school and staffroom were audiotaped.

The observations of science lessons were conducted on two separate days, within the same week, wherever possible. We took a running account of the science lesson as it took place, noted contextual information and time when activities changed, and made a narrative account of the lesson. Our understandings of science and language teaching built up from previous experience and reading and from meetings and discussions among members of the research team served as general background for conducting the observations. A checklist based on immersion teaching strategies described by Snow (1987, 1989) was also developed to assist in the observations of language teaching in the immersion classrooms. Documents such as classroom resources, student materials, and assignments were requested from the classroom teacher to complete the data set.

Teachers were interviewed for approximately 90 minutes after at least one classroom observation had been completed so that classroom activities could provide context for the interviews. A 20 minute student interview was also conducted with a small group of four students chosen according to random selection procedures.

Analysis

Research team members reviewed and completed field notes and recorded and amplified observations as soon as possible after each visit. In addition, we listened to the audiotaping of the classroom lessons, reviewed interview tapes, field notes, and documents collected, and made initial summaries of the school and classroom observations and the teacher and student interviews. Transcriptions of the interviews were also made and a complete case record for each classroom was assembled. We conducted ongoing analysis of the data, as we reflected, refined perceptions, and gained further insights as the study progressed. This is consistent with qualitative methodology, where the process of data collection and analysis is recursive and dynamic (Lincoln & Guba, 1985).

For the preparation of the case studies for immersion classrooms,[2] all the data were first reviewed, including notes, observations, classroom recordings, interview transcriptions, and case profiles for each teacher. A common format was developed for writing the cases; each case begins with a descriptive summary of the classroom observations and summary comments based on the observations triangulated with the interview and other data collected. These are followed by a presentation of the interview data structured around the following topics: science pedagogy, language pedagogy, and integration of language and science. All the data collected guided the interpretations and judgements on these topics, using triangulation to confirm, disconfirm or check the interpretations and decisions.

Case Study Results

Case 1: Claudette

Classroom observation

Claudette's first class began with a review of cellular structure. Students were asked to work in pairs and formulate questions for the review. They asked their questions of the class, with individual students volunteering to answer them. Claudette provided overall structure to the class, guiding students, summarizing major points orally and on the board, and encouraging them to extend their questioning and justify their answers. The interaction took place entirely in French.

At one point, a student asked the question: 'Qu'est-ce que c'est le tissu le plus important?' The teacher asked all students to think about the answer to this question, telling them that they would have to justify their responses. She allowed them to discuss their ideas amongst themselves first which, as she later explained, gave students a chance to try out their ideas and gain confidence. A class discussion followed. During this time, the teacher kept students' interest and participation at a high level by asking them whether they thought there was only one good answer to this question. Opportunity for students to reason, share ideas, communicate in French, and be comfortable with the view that there is 'no one right answer' were all provided in this part of the review, which appears to have taken place quite spontaneously.

The second part of the lesson was a lab in which students studied the skin. Working in pairs, they made observations of their own skin tissue with a magnifying glass and drew and labelled what they observed on a large sheet of paper. After about three minutes, Claudette asked them about their observations, repeating their answers and commenting that the word for 'pores' was the same in French as in English. She then had students outline their hands on the paper and identify the various parts. The children played with words like dessus/dessous. They then continued with the next part of the lab, which was to test how skin tissue reacts to pressure.

The children seemed to be quite engrossed in this activity, observing carefully as they probed their partner's hand with a toothpick and recording their observations. They talked to one another freely, sometimes in French, sometimes in English, a frequently observed practice in immersion classrooms. After the class, Claudette commented that it was unfortunate there was no time for students to compare the results of their testing and discuss what they had found.

Summary comments

Claudette appeared to combine a didactic, structured approach to science teaching with a more open, discovery-oriented approach. The blend she made of teacher structure and student centredness was reflected in the physical arrangement of her classroom. Students' desks were arranged along the sides and back of the room, creating a large open area in the middle and front. This arrangement allowed attention to be focused on the teacher when necessary but it also favored student interaction and created a forum for communication, as students could all see one another.

In the classes observed, students had many opportunities to use French productively and communicate with one another. These opportunities appeared to arise inherently out of what was being learned and out of the discourse community the teacher created in the classroom rather than from any specific attempt to encourage productive language use. Students used a range of language functions (for example, relate, reason, hypothesize, predict) and they seemed able to handle the complex linguistic structures needed for talking about science. In addition, they appeared to have a good control of scientific vocabulary in French. They spoke French in the non-native fashion typical of immersion students and sometimes used English, but they were at ease in talking about science in French and had much to say.

It was difficult to separate any specific strategies Claudette used to promote language learning in the classroom from what might be equally construed as promoting science learning. Little attention seemed to be paid to code-related aspects of language through such means as error correction or explicit grammar or vocabulary teaching. With respect to immersion instructional strategies, one can broadly say that Claudette promoted both the receptive and productive aspects of language. One can also say that her classes broadly reflected Lindfors' (1980) description of an effective 'using language to learn' class, as well as the 'ideal learning community' described by Anderson (1987). Let us now turn to the interview data to see how Claudette's views and comments might help us understand her practice and contribute to our understanding of language/subject matter integration.

Interview data

In one section of the interview, I (Elaine) selected one of the prominent features that I thought reflected the language pedagogy observed and asked Claudette about that. I also asked her to comment on anything else in her language pedagogy she would like to talk about. Since I had noticed that Claudette frequently reformulated and repeated the questions students had asked of one another in the review, I asked her to comment on this as an aspect of her pedagogy. Our discussion went as follows:

Interviewer   Today we noticed especially in the beginning when you were reviewing with students, that you reformulated the students' questions or repeated them fairly frequently. Is that something that you would want to comment on? Was that something that you were doing specifically?

Claudette   I do it all the time to teach them to paraphrase.

Interviewer   So was that a linguistic objective?

Claudette   I just do it all the time because I think that paraphrasing is important. It's important in research. It's important in understanding. You need to be able to paraphrase all the time, so I try to provide a continual modelling, and also helping them to hear their own thoughts right back and say 'That's what I meant' or 'No, that's not.'

Because the paraphrasing often seemed to be providing a more correct model of language to students (for example, a student's question 'Qu'est-ce qui fait le travail du membrane?' was paraphrased by the teacher as 'Qu'est-ce que le membrane fait dans son travail?' and 'Qu'est-ce que le tissu est responsable?' was paraphrased as 'Que fait le tissu?'), I probed further to find out how important paraphrasing was as a linguistic objective.

Interviewer   You seemed to be clarifying, getting them to clarify their thought, and also providing a more correct model of language by restructuring certain questions. Was that your objective?

Claudette   I do it more for the purpose of helping them understand the French language, as a modelling of a tool that I think is crucial, because when they read and they don't understand, they can paraphrase in their minds. I'm hoping. I have no real idea that they are doing it, but that's my underlying goal there. I do it in every subject.

Thus, while I had supposed that the teacher may have intended to provide a more correct model of language through her paraphrasing, her responses suggest that this was not her primary purpose. She used paraphrasing to provide students with a mirror they could use in checking their thoughts (i.e. to allow the child to negotiate meaning with him/herself) and at the same time to promote a general learning strategy or tool that could be used in understanding French.

I then asked Claudette whether there were other teaching strategies for promoting language learning in the science class that she would like to talk about, and she immediately mentioned vocabulary. This was fortunate because I was impressed with the variety and range of the students' scientific vocabulary both in the class that I had observed and in the interview conducted with a group of her students after the class. In addition, I had noticed a few cases in class where the teacher gave the students the meaning of a word without much elaboration or explanation or without writing it on the board. Claudette told me that she believed in a naturalistic approach to vocabulary teaching and found that students learned scientific vocabulary much better if she used the words in context. This allowed students to infer meaning, play with words, and use them when they were ready.

'I don't put any stress on words. I don't expect them to learn four syllable words. I have found that when I do, it doesn't work . . . If I provide them with the word and at least they're seeing it an awful lot of times, and that word begins to make sense. And what is it somebody told me one time? You have to see a word or read it 60 times before you grasp the meaning and begin to use it. So I lean more toward using it myself . . . So it's more giving them an awareness of the word rather than expecting them to regurgitate. And what I found in retrospect using both ways, one expecting them to know and insisting that they do and the other, just kind of using it, I find they use it more when I just don't put that pressure on them. I'll find it in their vocabulary . . . I couldn't believe it. That was really astounding to me, you know. They were saying "conjoncteur" and they were playing with it. Whereas I'm sure if I had said "I expect you to know these words", that pressure would have been enough for them to say: "I can't. It's too long. It's too big". This way, they were going, "That doesn't sound right". They were correcting themselves. So I find they use them more. They feel more comfortable with the science terminology when I don't put an emphasis on it.'

When I asked Claudette whether this gave the students any difficulties, she replied in the affirmative, saying that it took more time. She also indicated that she accepted the need for time in learning because she had a broader objective of having students connect the word to a meaning:

'Oh, sure it does. I think it's a matter of time. I think it's a matter of allowing them to get familiarized with it. I find in the actual language, they have so much to learn . . . I think if we had smaller objectives, like just my objective of them connecting the word to a sense, rather than memorizing the word, if they can see it being used and talk about it and say that's "conjonctif" and that's "conjoncteur", that the lack of pressure enables them simply to learn it because they want to, because it's the proper word, like you would say "table" for a table and not a chair. So there's no real pressure there. And then learning how to spell it and you have to give me this definition for it.'

Her closing comment suggests that she did have expectations of her students ultimately being able to define certain words and spell them correctly, but she had broader goals for language learning (i.e. what she called 'smaller objectives . . . connecting the word to a sense') and was willing to take the time to let this happen. As we talked, Claudette reiterated the need for children to become familiar with using words in science:

'In science, what I try to do with the vocabulary is just make it familiar, just use it. "Cellule", they know what that is. "Membrane", you use the word and they go, "Oh, yeah". They can see the exterior part of the "cellule" and that's the "membrane". I expect them to know it, but only after we use it an awful lot and talk about it and review it.'

In response to this, I asked her whether this was the reason she had students formulate their own questions in the first part of the class we had seen. The intimate connection between language and content learning became clear in her answer:

Interviewer Is that why you had them asking questions at the beginning rather than your asking them?

Claudette Yes.

Interviewer That was to promote their use of language?

Claudette Promote the use of language and also force them to think about what they've learned. To form a question, you need to have a learning.

Claudette's comments on her language pedagogy were reflected in some of her comments on her science pedagogy. For example, her belief in student experience as the way to learning and a willingness to take the time to allow that to happen came up when I asked her to talk about the experiment she had had students do in the class we observed.

'Well, my attitude is that I go in wanting them to take out a certain learning . . . And by experimenting, I'm hoping that they will understand the concept I'm trying to get across though they may not have picked it up on their own. And also I'm depending on the fact that they are learning a tremendous amount more that I may never know and that is wonderful for them. And the actual doing and exploring, I feel, is also a builder of self-esteem because the children realize they know already a lot of what's being said. They can feel that "Hey, I knew that", rather than "I'm being told that". . . The only problem I have with it is that it takes forever. That will make three lessons on skin that I'll have gone through in three days, where if I had just taken the sheet and said, "This is your skin", it would have taken me 40 minutes. Sometimes I just run out of time and have gone maybe through half of what I told you I intend to, because it takes that time.'

In addition, some of her subsequent comments in which she revealed that she was struggling with the dilemma of 'what to teach' in science suggested that she distinguished clearly between a fact and a relation or underlying objective, just as she did when she talked about vocabulary:

'Is it important to know the distance of a planet from the earth or just that one's further from the other? Where do you differentiate in what the kids really need to know, and especially the laws of science? I have a girlfriend working on her doctorate and according to her, there aren't that many laws of science that really need to be learned in order to build on and understand the more complex ones. So where are they? Which ones are they, right? And my advice . . . would be not to spend so much time and focus on facts especially because they change so much.'

Finally, her response to the question asking her whether there were any other teaching strategies or approaches to teaching science that she would like to talk about reflected an open-ended approach to teaching with considerable responsibility placed on students. She said that she had been trying to get students to devise their own questions and experiments and recounted her difficulties and disappointments:

'I would try to give them time and say what would you like to find out about water? What would you like to try with water? It wouldn't work out. What wouldn't work about it? They didn't know what to do, or they would sit and put it aside and not bother, and that kind of concerned me; their actual interest, where does that wanting to know go? Where did that curiosity go? I had all kinds of things they could have done with it, all kinds of substances they could have mixed with it, and it just wasn't happening. It's almost like if they're not told what to do exactly, they don't know what to do, and that kind of concerned me, especially in science where I view it as learning about what's around you and just exploring, finding out.'

As we shall see in some of her comments on integration, this approach can provide a rich basis for integrating language and science.

Claudette's views on integration provide further insights into the relationships between language and science teaching. For example, when asked whether she incorporated language arts objectives into her science classes, she said that she did through research, reading (for example, books related to the body), and the vocabulary they learned. She also mentioned that when students had written projects, she used the editing process with them:

> 'We'll stop and if they'd written a project, we'll go through the editing process and I won't just accept anything. We'll have to edit it.'

Her subsequent comments suggest that she seems to derive objectives for language arts out of the science activities rather than vice versa:

> 'Occasionally, I do spelling lists, and occasionally we'll look at some science words if I think they can spell them, if they're not too difficult, or words that we've discovered, like Friday, we're going to do the touch activity. They might say, "How do you say smooth in French?" We'll find it and that will go on the word list.'

One of the questions I asked was whether she felt the science curriculum lent itself to teaching language. At first, she said she did not think so but then commented that the teacher needed to find ways to integrate and came out with a stream of ideas on how this could be done, mentioning in particular creative writing and drama:

> 'Again, it depends on the subject. I think it's not conducive to it. I think the teacher needs to find ways to integrate it. For example, the body. They may become a person who can be zapped by an epsilon ray and shrinks to microscopic and then it's swallowed by a person and travels through the body, you know, tell me about your travels . . . There are ways and things that you can draw out, I guess, and have some creative writing happening and maybe some drama.'

She closed by implying that formal links between language arts and science were more difficult, suggesting why she had originally replied that she did not feel the science curriculum particularly lent itself to teaching language arts:

> 'But what I'm thinking of is, say, finding a story that will go with what you're doing, a novel other than science fiction and planets, but there again, I don't find it as related as it can be.'

I asked her about the oral aspects of language, and her reply reflected what I had seen in her class. It also reflected the teacher's emphasis on the imaginative and speculative in science:

> 'The discussion component, sure, if you're experimenting and talking things through and asking for their ideas and letting them imagine and predict. One question that I will come to, you probably won't be here, is: "Imagine life without skin. What would it be like?" Some things they brought up today when I allowed them to just kind of answer. They asked me, "Well, which is the right answer?" My answer was, "Who

cares?" basically . . . so when I can manage to create an atmosphere of anything goes, just give me your thoughts, then we can come out with some really neat things.'

I commented that the discussion was quite interesting and that children seemed to be quite comfortable in that kind of open situation, and she indicated that this had taken some time to develop in the children, suggesting that having students speculate and be inventive was a general objective for her science teaching.

'It took a long time to develop that in those kids. Even now they're still kind of taking a chance when it comes to just inventing.'

Thus, opportunities for productive language use appear to arise out of her view of science as inquiry and speculation rather than specific attempts to promote oral language skills.

Summary of case 1

In Claudette's classes, students were engaged in both 'doing' science and talking about it, not only to the teacher but to one another. The classroom was a communicative arena, in which all shared their knowledge and developed their understandings. While the teacher had specific learning objectives and structured her classes accordingly, she also encouraged students to speculate and be comfortable with the view that there might be 'no right answer' to some questions. Students had many opportunities to use French productively and to communicate with one another, and they used a wide variety of language functions and structures. These opportunities (and the language products they created) appeared to arise inherently out of what was being learned and out of the discourse community the teacher had created in the classroom rather than out of any specific attempt to foster productive language skills. In observing Claudette's classes, it was difficult to isolate any specific strategies used to promote language learning that might not be equally construed as promoting science learning. Rather, language and science were fused into a unified whole.

The interview data suggested that Claudette felt it was important for students to learn science through their own discovery and she was willing to allow the time for this to happen. She appeared to hold broader learning goals firmly in view and did not let more specific objectives override these (a 'keep your eyes on the prize' approach). In addition, she was trying to encourage a more open-ended approach to learning with greater responsibility placed on students. Her views on language teaching reflected a similar emphasis on the importance of experience, the need for time in learning, and an appeal to broader over more specific objectives. These commonalities suggest a fundamental unity in her approach to teaching; and it is perhaps because of this that when she spoke about integration, she could describe many ways in which what she did in science naturally promoted productive language use.

Case 2: Michel

Classroom observation

The class observed was a half-hour class on the topic of force. It was traditional in its arrangement and in the way it was taught. Students were seated at their desks, which were arranged in five neat rows facing the chalkboard. The teacher stood at the front of the room in front of the board, chalk in hand and ready to go. He began the class by announcing that they were going to do science and asked students to get out their textbooks. However, the textbooks were not used at all during the class.

The first part of the class consisted of a 15 minute question and answer session in which students were asked to provide examples of force. With the exception of about two interchanges of a few short sentences, students answered in a word or a phrase. Michel spoke very clearly and was a good model of French, but he elaborated very little and did not encourage students to expand their answers. He repeated or rephrased what they said, wrote the answers on the board, and had students take notes.

At one point, Michel suddenly announced that he wanted students to take five minutes to draw a cartoon illustrating force. There was no transition or summing up of the first part of the lesson; students seemed surprised and asked questions about what they were to do. Michel circulated among students as they were drawing, answering their occasional questions, including responding to a few students who still were unsure about the task. I looked up at the chalkboard and noticed that he had erased everything he had written. After approximately eight minutes and when students had finished their drawings, Michel initiated the third and final part of the class by announcing that he would like students to give him examples of force in nature. This part of the class continued in the same question and answer format as the first part. The following excerpt illustrates:

| Teacher | Bon, si je joue avec la nature. Donnez-moi des exemples de force dans la nature, des exemples de force dans la nature. Quelles sont des forces dans la nature? Parfois je peux même utiliser le terme phénomène. |
| Student | Les vents. |

Teacher	Les vents, d'accord. OK, autre chose?
Student	L'éclair.
Teacher	L'éclair. Autre chose?
Student	La force de la gravité.
Teacher	Oui. Je veux quelque chose d'encore plus spécifique de qu'est-ce qu'on entend par la force. Oui, la force de gravité si je saute comme ça, d'accord.
Student	La pluie.
Teacher	La pluie. Je veux quelque chose de plus sensationnel. Dans la nature, je veux quelque chose de sensationnel.
Student	Terrestre.
Teacher	Ça peut être . . .
Student	La formation des continents quand . . . [inaudible on tape].
Teacher	Oui, d'accord. Ç'est bien d'avoir pensé à ça.
Student	Tremblement de terre.
Teacher	Oui, tremblement de terre. Autre chose?

Michel's prompts suggest that he wanted to elicit student responses falling under his pre-determined categories. When a student's response did not conform to what he wanted, he redirected it. For example, to move students away from providing examples of terrestrial force, he prompted them as follows: 'OK, go out of the earth now; go elsewhere'. A student answered: 'The rotation of the planets'. He acknowledged this answer and wrote it on the board. This was not really the response he seemed to want, however, for his subsequent prompt suggested that he wanted them to talk about water before talking about the sky. 'Ça se trouve dans l'eau', he hinted. A student answered: 'Waves'. Another student then brought up the topic of the Bermuda triangle. This was not discussed, however, for now it was time to talk about the sky. The style of prompt was similar: 'OK, let's go up into the sky. What is there in the sky?' This prompted the same kind of one-word answers elicited throughout the lesson.

With the same suddenness with which he had introduced the art activity earlier, he asked if students had heard of Stephen W. Hawking. One child volunteered an answer. The teacher then asked students to see if they had the book *A Brief History of Time* at home and gave them their homework, which was to find some documentation and write one page on the Bermuda triangle and black holes.

Summary comments

Contrary to the difficulty I had experienced in Claudette's class in separating strategies for language learning from those for science learning, I was able to isolate a few specific strategies that seemed to be geared toward language learning in Michel's class. These were purposely making a mistake in spelling when writing on the board and asking students whether the spelling was correct (if they didn't know, they were encouraged to look it up in the dictionary) and occasionally encouraging students to look up words in their dictionaries. Little attention seemed to be paid to error correction or explicit grammar teaching, but this was the case in all of the immersion classes I observed.

The verbal sparseness of Michel's class was a striking contrast to the verbal richness I had experienced in Claudette's class. While Michel spoke clearly and in this was a good model of French, he elaborated very little and did not encourage students to expand their answers. Students rarely gave more than one word or one phrase answers. There was little, if any, interaction among them. All attention was directed toward the teacher, toward the content categories that he appeared to want to elicit; these were mechanically engraved on the board and dutifully recorded by students.

With respect to the immersion instructional strategies described earlier in the literature review, one can broadly say that Michel only weakly promoted the receptive aspects of language and did little to promote the productive aspects. Characteristics of Lindfors' effective 'using language to learn' class and Anderson's 'ideal learning community' described earlier were notable for their absence. Active children and ideas make up these communities. Passive children and carefully categorized scientific facts made up Michel's community during my observations, and the textbook and the chalkboard were its master. Let us turn now to the interview data to see how Michel's views and comments can help us understand the observations and contribute to our understanding of language/subject matter integration.

Interview data

Michel's interview data were at first difficult to interpret since his professed views about science and science pedagogy did not appear to be consistent with the pedagogy I had observed in his classes. However, further analysis suggested that he may have been paying lip-service to a 'pedagogically correct' view of science as inquiry, and he often appealed to the constraints of science teaching seemingly to defend why he did not teach that way. The following examples taken from different parts of the interview illustrate:

'We don't do enough of that [i.e. observing and discovering] and it's lack of time. There's only so many minutes in a day, days in a week. It's unfortunate.'

'Where we have to maximize and capitalize is to offer the children more of an opportunity to explore . . . Give them more complex things, and of course, because we don't have a lab and because we don't have the materials, we can't push their brain power into expanding their knowledge.'

'Let them go into the schoolyard with a bunch of materials and build something. Apply these laws, try to defy them, whatnot. I don't have the resources for that. I don't have the space. All this comes back to what I said initially, you know, it's that hands-on. Let them discover . . . I think that's what we're lacking.'

Michel described the class I had seen as a brainstorming class in which he was trying to get the children thinking. He said that lecturing was not the right way to approach this because you had to engage students and have interaction.

'This is the introduction that I'm doing. This morning for the introduction you brainstorm with them and you get them more viable, you know, because you lose them if you're just going to go there and just lecture. Forget it. It doesn't work . . . You have to engage. Anyway, it's no fun just standing up there and just talking. That's ridiculous. That's not called teaching. So you need that interaction, so you have to get them going. Gradually, they do all the thinking. You don't.'

When I asked if this was a typical science class, he said it was, saying that he liked 'an awful lot of participation from them'. My experience in the class suggested that his view of engagement, interaction, and participation was different from mine. The interaction was entirely teacher-initiated and controlled, and there was little interaction among students.

When asked what kinds of things he did in his science classes, Michel mentioned a variety of activities, including videos, research, discussions, and some lab work. As the extensive note-taking he had had his students do was a salient feature of the classes observed, I asked him whether this was typical of his teaching. He replied that this was part of their high school training. As the following comment suggests, he considered this to be recording and useful as a reminder for students of what they had done rather than as a strategy to get them to do any higher order analysing or synthesizing of information.

Michel   Yes, that's part of high school training. They're taught very very early in grade 7, first week in September, they learn that when I speak or if I write on the board, that's part of what they should be recording. And as they are recording, some of what I give them may be pertinent and that may trigger, when they reread their notes whenever, to spark a question or not, so they have to write that down.

Interviewer   Yes, they seem to be quite adept at it. What do you have them do with those notes?

Michel   That's part of studying.

Interviewer   So that they will refer to that?

Michel   Refer to that and also . . . all very good students every night, they reread that, of course, very diligently. You see, and that should kind of spark, and sometimes it does, you know, sometimes just two minutes before I start. "OK, come on now, we're taking this page and we're going to be dealing with this. Now what did we do yesterday?" All right, so they'll just glance over. And sometimes I'll say, "Well, you said this, what do you think now? I've come up with this". OK, great, and then it starts with a discussion. But it's to help them out.

I asked whether he used any other teaching strategy that he would like to talk about, and at first he said that he didn't. He then said that he did not like using overheads. As he put it and as I had experienced in the classroom, 'I like my blackboard'. I commented that he seemed quite conscientious about using the board and asked whether he was doing it because he felt it was important for the students' note-taking. After replying affirmatively to my question, Michel spontaneously led me into the subject of language pedagogy, saying that his writing on the board was also a mini-tool for learning French and giving as an example his making a spelling error to see whether students were paying attention or not:

Michel   . . . and also, seeing that it's done in French, well then, it acts as a mini-tool often. For instance, times that I purposely make an error, a spelling error, to see how much they're with me or not. For instance, "tiroir".

Interviewer   Yes, I noticed that.

Michel   Right away that dictionary is not foreign. I want it to be literally affixed to your arm as an extension of your brain. I want you to use it at all times regardless. It's not only utilized for composition purposes. It's all the time. So I purposely do it because they're allergic to the dictionary. They do not like going to the dictionary to check. I purposely do that. What would be a synonym? OK, let's go to the thesaurus because they have these in French so it's no problem. And also it's for spelling. You have to think of the visual child. There are children who can only learn that way, by seeing. You know they can hear, but it doesn't catch as well. We have to contend for all the kids, all types of learners as much as possible. You don't get them all. You try.

Thus, it appears that one way Michel integrates language and science teaching is to train students to use the dictionary to check his spelling errors and verify the meaning of words. These seem to be artificially imposed with little real purpose other than to foster a disposition for students to use the dictionary.

Later in the interview, I asked Michel whether he used any other teaching strategies for promoting language learning in his science class that he would like to talk about, and he again mentioned promoting the use of the dictionary. He also said that he insisted on correct spelling and syntax, so that students wouldn't compartmentalize their learning of French.

'The dictionary, that's basically as specific as I will be. A classic question when they're writing a test or when they're writing up an experiment or whatnot, their observations or conclusions or whatever, they always say, "Does the spelling count?" I say, "You're darn right it counts". I have to be very careful with the syntax because children like to . . . compartmentalize, children are very much like that too. So what I try as much as possible is to see if they're . . . Learning is nothing but building bridges.'

Thus, he sees the science classroom as a way to reinforce language learning from language arts, but these appear to remain at the level of reinforcing technical skills. His use of the buzzword 'building bridges' in this context revealed a similar limited view as his previous uses of words like 'brainstorming', 'engagement' and 'interaction'.

Michel's replies to the questions on integration further reflected how he viewed the possibilities of science for promoting language learning. When asked whether he had students in his science periods engage in activities that met objectives in both language arts and science curricula, he replied that he did, mentioning accuracy and terminology as important.

'That is totally incidental, OK. I still demand a complete sentence, and I do want the correct word. You're dealing with descriptions; you're writing down your observations; you have to be as accurate as possible, so your terminology is very important here.'

I also asked if and how he fostered the different language skills in the science class in order to prompt him to speak more broadly about the opportunities for language use his science classes might provide. However, he again referred to technical skills, in this case punctuation:

'Yes, but I do it in a very non-threatening way, how's that? It's very subtle. I don't go around and say, "Oh, you forgot your period here". You dock marks for a period. "No. Just be careful. I think there's something missing here".'

To probe further, I asked whether he felt that the science curriculum lent itself to teaching language arts. In reply, he told me that interest in the scientific world might spark an interest for students to read science, whether fiction or non-fiction. However, this appears to be left up to the individual student, rather than arising out of the teacher's attempt to encourage this kind of reading.

Summary of case 2

In contrast to the previous teacher, Claudette, Michel had a didactic approach to teaching science. While he was willing to begin with students' knowledge in introducing the textbook material, the lack of any discussion or exploration of the students' answers and his tendency to want to direct their responses to certain predetermined categories suggest that this knowledge would not be used in any meaningful way as a basis for their learning. The teacher asked for a list, the students gave him a list, the teacher wrote the list on the board, and the students took notes.

Michel's classes were a good illustration of how a didactic science pedagogy translates into a didactic language pedagogy. While the teacher spoke clearly and was in this a good model of French, he elaborated very little and did not encourage students to expand their answers. Students rarely gave more than one word or one phrase answers, and there was little, if any, interaction among them. All attention was directed toward the teacher, toward the content categories that he wanted to elicit; these were mechanically engraved on the chalkboard and dutifully recorded in the students' notes. Contrary to my experience in Claudette's class, however, I was able to isolate some specific strategies directed at promoting students' language learning in Michel's class. These were of a rather minor sort and appeared to be arbitrary insertions rather than arising inherently out of the teaching of the subject matter.

While Michel professed to see learning science as a process of discovery, his views were not congruent with my observations of his teaching. He appeared to be paying lip-service to a 'pedagogically correct' view of science as inquiry, and he often appealed to the constraints of science teaching seemingly to defend why he did not teach that way. In addition, my experience in his classes suggested that he may have a rather limited view of the words he used to describe them; in any case, there was a wide gap between how he construed words like 'brainstorm', 'engage', 'interact', and 'participate' and the way I construed them. His description of note-taking as a process of recording, used as a reminder for students of what they had done rather than as a strategy to encourage them to do any higher order analyzing or synthesizing of information, left me with little reason to believe that he viewed learning other than as a passive process of receiving knowledge from the teacher or from the textbook, which sat symbolically on students' desks.

It is perhaps no coincidence that Michel talked about his language pedagogy in terms of technical skills, in which another important book, the dictionary, predominated. This focus became apparent also in his comments on integration, where he described the ways he reinforced technical skills like punctuation, spelling and use of correct terminology, with little mention of the rich occasions for language use that his science class might provide. Overall, Michel's comments on integration suggested that he saw his science class as a place to reinforce language 'usage' rather than language 'use'.

Let us turn now to our third teacher who provides a judicious combination of implicit and explicit attention to language flowing naturally out of the context of the science lesson.

Case 3: Jean Jacques

Classroom observation

The first lesson observed was a 45 minute lesson on plants. Before beginning, Jean Jacques told the observer that he wanted to introduce or review some of the vocabulary and concepts to be developed in the unit, saying that he wanted to let students draw on their previous experience and realize that they already had considerable knowledge of the subject. He began the lesson by writing a list of 13 words on the board (e.g. *organisme, racines, spores, algues*) and asking students to explain some of them, telling them that they could refer to their notebooks if they wanted to.

After eliciting a few simple definitions and examples of the words on the list, he questioned students on a variety of topics, referring to students' posters and drawings that were displayed around the classroom. Within a period of about 20 minutes, he got students to identify the parts of a plant, explain the function of roots and how carbon dioxide was made, think about the effect of gravity on plants, engage in a discussion on the need to preserve our trees, and discuss photosynthesis.

Jean Jacques paraphrased or summarized students' responses and ideas and repeated questions using different structures and vocabulary. Students made grammatical errors, most of which were ignored by the teacher, who accepted and built on students' replies. Jean Jacques then briefly discussed the topic of photosynthesis with students and then returned to the word list on the board. A student's attempt to explain the word *algues* led to an examination of the word *microscopique*. The following is a transcript of this part of the lesson:

Teacher	Une plante microscopique, qu'est-ce que ça veut dire une plante microscopique? Microscopique [writing the word on the board] voilà, il y a un mot que vous connaissez très, très bien dans 'microscopique'. Qui peut me donner un mot dedans que vous connaissez très, très bien.
Student 1	J'ai une [pause].
Teacher	Tu as [pause].
Student 1	Micro.
Teacher	Ah?
Student 1	Micro.
Teacher	'Micro' veut dire quoi?
Student 1	Microscope.
Student 2	[calls out, giving the answer] Petit.
Teacher	Très bien, Marie, 'micro' veut dire 'petit'. Alors, qui a dit micro?
Student	Microscope.
Teacher	Microscope. OK, je mets ça au tableau et vous allez m'expliquer. Moi, je ne sais rien, moi [students' giggling heard on tape]. OK, Marie a trouvé quoi? 'Micro', n'est-ce pas? Et maintenant ça reste, vous avez trouvé un autre mot avec ça?
Student	Microscope.

Teacher	Scope. Et puis on a fait microscopique, ça . . . qu'est-ce que . . . si j'utilise ça: J'ai quelque chose mais c'est microscopique . . .
Student	Tu dois avoir microscope.
Teacher	Non mais qu'est-ce que c'est? C'est très [pause].
Student	Petit.
Student	C'est si petit que tu dois avoir [pause].
Teacher	Tu dois avoir . . .
Student	Microscope.
Teacher	Maintenant y a-t-il quelqu'un dans la classe qui ne sait pas qu'est-ce que c'est un microscope?
Student	[Laughing] Je ne sais pas.
Teacher	Très, très bien, tout le monde sait . . . microscope. Et vous allez observer quoi?
Student	Cellules.
Teacher	On va enlever des cheveux de Jean, et on va voir les cellules de ces cheveux [students' giggling and bantering heard on tape].
Teacher	Bon, qu'est-ce qui arrive . . . supposez, tout le monde regarde ici, si j'avais [?] mis sous le microscope, qu'est-ce que tu penses qu'on va voir? Est-ce que les cheveux sont faits de cellules?
Student	Oui.
Teacher	Qui dit oui? Oui, chaque chose est faite de petites parties . . . de cellules. Et on aura plusieurs cellules qu'on peut voir peut-être, pour essayer. Et je pense qu'on peut voir . . .

As can be seen from the transcript, Jean Jacques encouraged his students to break up the word *microscopique* into syllables and look for words they knew in order to get at its meaning. He encouraged playfulness with language, getting them to see that *microscopique* meant something so small that you needed a microscope ('C'est si petit que tu dois avoir . . . microscope'). He also used this occasion to talk with students about what they could do with a microscope and had them use one to observe a strand of a student's hair. After they talked about their observations, he summarized for students:

'Et on a trouvé une plante maintenant qu'on peut seulement voir avec un microscope . . . il y a beaucoup d'autres plantes . . . qu'on ne peut pas voir avec les yeux comme çela. Elles sont partout. On peut seulement les voir avec le microscope. Ça nous dit quelque chose que les plantes ne sont pas toujours là comme on voit dehors, petit.'

After this discussion, Jean Jacques had a few students come to the front of the class to talk about the types of seeds they had planted, show their seedlings, and tell what had happened. Students were able to use the vocabulary that had been dealt with in the first part of the class. The teacher then returned again to the word list, dealing with the word '*spore*' by having students look the word up in a dictionary and then explaining the word with the aid of a student's drawing of a fern that was on the bulletin board.

Summary comments

This class was characterized by a rapid pace and quick changes of topics or activities. Jean Jacques elicited students' knowledge and views on many of the topics they were to cover in the unit and introduced them to the vocabulary they were learning. He frequently appealed to visuals, used students' experiences as a basis for talking, and highlighted words on the board. Much of the discussion appeared to arise spontaneously as students talked about the drawings they had done or as one topic led to another, and the teacher appeared to capitalize on these to draw out students' understanding of science concepts.

Listening and relistening to the classroom tapes, I could not help being struck by the enabling role the teacher played in encouraging students to express themselves in French. His frequent references to their posters and drawings which contained some of the plant vocabulary provided a useful visual framework around which to talk about many of the topics. When students were unable to think of a French word and there was a related English word, he encouraged them to use the English and then pointed out the relationship. When appropriate, he also encouraged them to go to the dictionary to find the meaning themselves. And he encouraged them to use their word analysis skills in the mini-lesson on *microscopique*.

Interview data

A discussion about language pedagogy came up early and quite spontaneously in the interview with Jean Jacques. In talking about his academic background, he mentioned that he had studied linguistics, pointing out its benefits in developing logical thought as well as one's understanding of how the child reasons:

'These courses in linguistics show you how to reason and you know where to get to. Even when I took phonology, semantics, phonetics and all this, you see how the child reasons.'

He continued, describing enthusiastically how he taught French verbs by having students infer rules from a large amount of observational data:

'I have a special way to teach French verbs. In French we have about 12,000 different verbs. You are not going to have teachers hand out these sheets with kids conjugating verbs. They become like robots. And they are not learning. If you teach them to observe, it's the scientific approach again. From this observation what do you find out? All the ER verbs, you show them that you add ER verbs, and then they write the rule.'

In talking, he revealed how he guided students, allowing them to trust their own implicit knowledge and rely on their judgments of sound, rather than on analytic procedures:

'We discuss it. We work together to make sure they know it. They get confused because they are English (anglophone). And the more they read, they become more aware of the different tenses that are collected in their heads. Does it sound good to your ears? That usually makes the judgement. Then we keep working on it.'

As previously mentioned in the summary comments, a striking feature of Jean Jacques' pedagogy was the the enabling role he played in getting students to express themselves in French. As he pointed out in the interview:

'Even yesterday, when you were sitting in science class, they knew the word in English and I just sit and wait for them to dig in and look for that. So I allow some English words and then the French will come. There is a problem with expression because they know it in English.'

When asked to talk about the strategy he had used to get students to break down the word *microscopique*, he explained that he taught students how to break down words and also encouraged them to look up words in a dictionary, seeing these as 'very good training' but also emphasizing the fun quality of it ('it becomes like a game').

When asked whether he felt there were any differences between teaching children in their first language and teaching them in immersion, he again used the word 'training', suggesting its importance in his teaching:

'You have the language barrier there, and you have to train your kids in French immersion to acquire those words.'

His juxtaposition of the two words 'train' and 'acquire' in the context of learning were interesting, for they reflect the dual approaches to language teaching observed in his classroom. Later in the interview he summarized his approach to vocabulary, using language which reflected how similar the terms he used to describe his language and science teaching were:

Jean Jacques   If you just learn words for the sake of learning words, it becomes very boring.

Interviewer   So these are ways you've devised for them to practice using the words.

Jean Jacques   That's right, and then they would be writing it [the word] down. It has to be complete. They have to have experiments, observation, playing with it.

When asked if he used any other strategies for promoting language learning in his science classes, he mentioned composition writing, indicating that he saw this as a way of developing logical thought and reminding me of the earlier link he had made between linguistics and logical thought:

> 'When they are writing something about science in their notebooks, it is composition writing. They have the words and the vocabulary and then here the language will change a little bit because it's more scientific language in there, thinking, putting thoughts together.

> I say think what you are doing precisely. Especially when you have to describe a procedure. What I teach them to do is start from Level A and before you reach Level C, go in order. Don't jump from here to there. And they have the tendency to do this. They like to type things into the computer because then you can move sentences here and there and what do you think. So while I am teaching them to program a computer, I am also teaching them creative writing, and the science is always there.'

With regard to integration, Jean Jacques said that he integrated as much and as often as possible, but was not specific, saying that students were reading, writing and acquiring new language all the time. While he had shown that training was an important aspect of learning language, this does not appear to be the only aspect of language learning for Jean Jacques. In his words:

> 'Language has to have saying and richness . . . Some teachers just go over the program and teach the curriculum. That is not the way you teach any subject. Even science, if we start talking about magnets, it might bring about something else.'

Jean Jacques' views on language pedagogy were reflected in his views on science pedagogy. When asked what science was, he mentioned the importance of observation; and remembering his earlier statement about allowing children to use the sound of words to guide them, I wondered if it was only coincidental that he mentioned listening as well as seeing as an important part of scientific observation:

'You can find it yourself because it's all around you . . . I teach them to listen to the woods and again that is observation and science. You can hear the insects and the birds. That will be one of our field trips. We are going to Ford's Lake, and they will study the trees and the plants.'

Jean Jacques said that he felt it was very important to use children's knowledge as the point of departure for his teaching. The following interchange shows how he promoted the dual goals of science and language learning by using students' activities and explanations as points of departure for the science lesson:

Jean Jacques Yesterday, I told them to pick up their books and start drawing what they want, but you have to explain to us what you draw.

Interviewer Is that what they did?

Jean Jacques They picked up their notebooks and chose for themselves what to draw and then explained. So it wasn't very complicated for them to understand.

Interviewer So you used that then?

Jean Jacques Yes, you take the information from them and then supply the information from them and what is missing.

He used experimentation and observation and involved the children.

Interviewer I saw you drawing on what they know and what you have done previously and then applying it.

Jean Jacques That's right, making it real and then applying it. They applied the force of gravity and then growing the seeds and then they drew, that so it's not something completely out.

When asked whether there were any other science teaching strategies he would like to talk about, he said that he felt experimentation and observation were very important. It was also noteable that he involved the children in a lot of discussion about 'how to do an experiment'.

The interview progressed to another section, in which Jean Jacques was asked to comment on two contrasting teacher scenarios played on tape. He emphasized the need for teachers to go on learning about science and talked about the approaches to teaching he had developed, in which rule-learning and application were important:

'If you have some knowledge of science, you don't stop at university. You keep reading. As a teacher, you are always in the process of learning. If you want to teach science, learn it; see what's going on. I have new methods in math too, because we do laws and principles, all sorts of things. Kids apply it in all kinds of languages. I told you about the verb; it's a scientific approach there too. You are making rules and laws just like the rules of knowledge. If you have the knowledge, you can apply it everywhere.'

His need to have objectives and outcomes for his teaching became apparent; since these were more in the way of overall objectives, they did not preclude the quick changes and turns which made his lessons difficult to observe.

Jean Jacques Say with plants before I teach them, I have to decide what I want them to learn from this and the outcome.

Interviewer What is your outcome for the unit on plants?

Jean Jacques OK. The final step will be a field trip to observe these plants and right now in the classroom environment when they do all their own work. I chose this because they are experimenting with seeds. So then afterwards they see what kind of environment they need to grow plants and then you talk about pest management and things like that, like 'Are these chemicals dangerous to you?' As long as you have a practical environment they are learning about. You don't want them to get sick also, so what happens is that you learn so many things. My outcome is to learn full observation right from the beginning of the seed. Here when they have it in a glass, they can see what is going on because at home they can't see it because it's in the ground. Then we'll try different things like whether plants can grow without light and we'll turn the lights off or can they grow with plastic over them.

Summary of case 3

Jean Jacques' class was characterized by a rapid pace and quick change of activities. He seemed to be able to glide into a succession of teaching interludes to the benefit of both science and language learning. His mini-lesson on the word *microscopique* shows him capitalizing on a 'teachable moment' in which he created a symphony of language and science teaching, using contextualization, personalization, humor and playfulness to rapidly tie scientific and lexical awareness and knowledge together.

Jean Jacques' interview data suggest that he had an almost missionary belief in the importance of rule-learning ('You are making rules and laws just like the rules of knowledge'). This was coupled with a belief in the need for the learner to build these rules from linguistic data, using their intuition to guide them ('And the more they read, they become more aware of the different tenses that are collected in their heads. Does it sound good to your ears? That usually makes the judgement'). And he saw his role as fostering both ('You have the language barrier there, and you have to train your kids in French immersion to acquire those words').

His patience in allowing students to 'dig in' and search for a word and the mini-lesson in which he encouraged students to use their word analysis skills will indeed probably strike a familiar note to many immersion teachers. While they may not show the same zeal for rule-learning as he, I hope that immersion teachers will see a mirror of themselves in Jean Jacques as he illustrates the dual role they play in coaching students to use the second language and training them in strategies that will help them 'acquire' it.

Let us now turn to the fourth and final case study. This case illustrates a teacher in the secondary grades concerned primarily with content teaching, working with students whom he feels have already acquired their second language.

Case 4: René

Classroom observation

This was a very small class of nine students held in a science lab classroom which was rather sterile in appearance – a few commercial posters, a table of elements on the bulletin board, not much color or life – so different from the elementary classes I had seen, I thought. René began the class with four to five minutes of social chatter and banter, and I immediately forgot the sterility of my surroundings! He then launched into the lesson, which consisted of a review of a chapter on chemical reactions in preparation for a test later in the week.

The class was a teacher-directed class, with the teacher asking questions and students answering. As he questioned, he gestured and moved about the room, sometimes stopping to explain a point or write on the board. René used the Socratic method throughout the class, hinting, probing, and prodding students until he seemed satisfied with their answers. I heard the word *pourquoi* used frequently. Students were allowed to look in their textbooks for information. Although many of the students' answers were a word or a sentence, René asked students to justify their answers and elicited some longer responses. The following excerpt is typical of the interchanges I heard; regrettably, it was difficult to hear the students' voices on the classroom tape, and so it was not possible to capture the longer responses.

Teacher	Marie, est-ce que tu peux me dire quel est un exemple de déplacement quotidien?
Student	Je sais.
Teacher	OK, Jean, tu sais, tu sais quoi?
Jean	Le, le rouille.
Teacher	La rouille. OK, c'est la rouille [pause] dans une automobile . . . déplace quoi? Quel chimique déplace un autre chimique?
Jean	. . . l'oxygène et le gaz . . . [answer inaudible on tape].
Teacher	'Oxygène' n'est pas sur ce tableau, Jean.
Jean	Le fer déplace, le fer déplace l'hydrogène.
Teacher	L'hydrogène dans le métal? dans l'acier?
Student	Hmm.
Teacher	Ça vous pose une difficulté.
Jean	Oui, mais c'est quelque chose que [inaudible on tape].
Teacher	Tu as raison mais tu ne sais pas pourquoi. Qu'est-ce qu'on place sur les rues? pendant l'hiver?
Jean	Le sel.
Teacher	Quel est un composant positif du sel?
Jean	Le sodium.
Teacher	Le sodium, mon dieu, le sodium remplace quoi?
Jean	Le fer.
Teacher	Le fer, c'est ça. Et ça cause la rouille . . . le fer fait une combinaison avec l'oxygène pour faire la rouille. Mais c'est libre à cause du déplacement de sodium pour le fer. Oui, OK, les deux arrivent en même temps. OK, Lise, ça va? [long pause] On dit que ces deux réactions sont exothermiques. Est-ce que ça veut dire que pendant l'hiver on peut se poser dans la voiture et qu'on [end of tape, side 1].

René frequently summed up, explained, and wrote formulas and explanations on the board. He used references to experiments students had done and to their everyday experiences to contextualize the material. French was used in the class throughout and the teacher spoke clearly and gestured a lot. There seemed to be little overt attention to language, except for the correction of gender for the word *rouille* (in preceding transcript) and a good-natured reminder to a student that he was using an anglicism ('Quel anglicisme!').

Summary comments

This was mainly a teacher-directed class, in which the teacher used the Socratic method of question and answer to get students to think about their experiments and to relate the ideas and concepts in the chapter being reviewed. The class was quite stimulating because of the energy René put into his questioning and because of his extensive probing for students' understandings. I was impressed by the way he got them to think about their experiments and draw on their experiences. Clarity of language and explanation gave students good language models, and requiring students to verbalize their understandings of the material gave them some opportunity to use language, although most of the discourse was in short phrases or sentences.

Interview data

When I asked him to talk about the science class I had observed, René said that he was trying to have students mentally review what they had learned. His description corresponded to my impressions of his teaching that day:

> 'What I was doing today was trying to have the students go back through their minds and go over all of the ideas and the experiments that we've done, and I wanted to get them to crystalize them in their own minds and put all the pieces together. It was really a summative class . . . It was all ideas and things that they had done before, and I was trying to get them to put all the cubbyholes together. In other words, I was trying to make sure that all the connections that I saw as important between this idea and that idea, A and B, were made, so I was going back over them. Tell me, where's the connection there. I was specifically going and trying to get them to put connections, and I was making the point of pulling them together. If they hadn't made one, I was showing them.'

René said that this was typical of his teaching, but mentioned also using a variety of other approaches, including experimentation and observation, 'semi-lecturing', group work, textbook reading, and oral presentations. I asked him to comment on his having students refer to an open textbook to review the material, and he again emphasized the importance of having students make their own connections between ideas:

> 'I wanted them to make the connections. I wanted to give them the connections as little as possible. I wanted them to succeed in finding

the answer. So that, to me, it was more the success, and being able to put the two things together, was more important than having to be able to dream it up out of memory, so that in this case, if they couldn't remember the name.'

René said he loved to teach science and loved to teach just about anything in science.

'You see, to me, physics is supremely exciting, so the piece that we do there is force and work and . . . I always go beyond what's in the book, just because I can't help myself.'

He mentioned genetics as one of the topics he most liked to teach because of the many ethical questions involved, and he talked about the excitement the topic engendered in students:

'And it also gets into the whole idea of genes and cross-matching, and they enjoy that too, and they go nuts on the one about recessive gene traits, dominant recessive gene traits. I get them to go home and do their whole family . . . They roar home . . . Everybody comes back with data . . . "Well my dad wasn't home but I phoned him, you know, and he's got hair on his fingers". So they all come back with that one. So that one's fun. You know, and it has a lot of long range open-ended questions in it, so probably that's the one I like the most, but I like them all. There isn't one I don't like.'

Later I asked him to talk about the place of the textbook in the science program, because both principal and department head had pointed out to me that the textbook was the same in French as in English, and René had shown the book to me at the beginning of my observation. René said that he used the text for a number of reasons. He thought it was a good text, students liked having a text, and parents were assured of equivalent content in French and English. He also said that having a reliable textbook facilitated teaching, but added that he also used his own resource materials.

I turned to the questions on language pedagogy, asking René first about his gesturing, which I had noticed had been quite extensive in the class I had seen. He said that this was not specific to his teaching in French; he gestured all the time, whether teaching immersion or English classes. He said that he did not do anything differently in immersion than he did in regular English classes, mentioning commonalities in planning and teaching strategies but leaving some openness for what actually happened in the classroom:

'So, there's virtually no difference . . . if I start off on a topic and we start off on a tangent, that may go anywhere, I mean, but then that's not planned, that just happens. If they start asking me questions about a certain thing, well, I'll just go with it and away we go. Again, we're going from the idea of, as long as you're finding out about something, fine . . . so, that's tactics. That's not strategy. Strategically, I approach them exactly the same.'

I asked if he would be using similar language, and he replied: 'Exactly'. He then thought for a moment and said that he told immersion students key words and phrases in English as well as in French because he wanted them 'to be able to cross-reference their minds'.

When I asked whether he thought there were any constraints to teaching French immersion, he said that students' linguistic abilities in French were not as good as in English. This made him think of a difference in the way he approached teaching science in immersion, namely that he took less for granted with immersion students and was more likely to ensure their comprehension of basic concepts or terminology before introducing new ones:

René I assume that they [English students] will know a certain term, or they will know this or that or the other thing. With the French immersion kids, I will question myself, do you know what this means? Because if I'm going to use this and talk about it, then you have to know what this means before I can talk about it. Otherwise, it makes no sense.

They've got to attach onto the movie that's going on in their mind. I make sure that that attachment is there. In other words, if I'm trying to attach piece M into their minds and piece M attaches onto piece K, then I make sure that piece K is there first, so that I will specifically, you know . . . 'You guys know what this means in French? You know how this fits? You've got this?' And then I'll go on . . . I don't think to do that. I just do that. I don't plan to do that. I don't write in my day book, make sure they understand this. When I get there I make sure, and if they need more explanation, then I give it to them, and then we go on.

Interviewer So it's verifying [slight pause].

René Verifying that they've got the base concept that I want to build above. Whereas in the English, I probably take it a little bit more for granted that they've got that base concept and then I start building, unless I start getting blank stares and go back and rebuild that.

When I asked him whether he integrated language arts and science objectives, René replied that he did, saying that this was 'on a low level' and mentioning grammar correction. He also mentioned that he had students do oral activities to get them to speak French:

> 'Yes, but on a low level. I correct their grammar, verbal and written, and there are times when I will specifically want them to do things, like oral reports and things like that because I want them to speak . . . Perhaps not the most important thing, but perhaps an equally important thing is the language arts component . . . I don't think it ever becomes the most important thing in a particular lesson, but at times it becomes co-important.'

As we talked further about integrating language and science, he made a very interesting observation, which indicated that he was conscious of promoting language learning in his immersion classes but not in English classes, even though he used the same kind of activities in the latter:

René   I've never thought of it in that way. Probably not, because, as I said, I really run the two courses almost exactly parallel and so I've never thought of it, you see. Because we're doing this in French, the thought comes to me, 'Well it's important that they speak, that they write, that they do this and that and the other thing.' That thought never comes to me in the English class, but I do exactly the same thing anyway, so the fact that it's important means that it's important, and it's equally in French as it is in English, so the language arts . . . I never think of it in the English class. I guess it's subliminal for me.

Interviewer But it's in your mind in French?

René   It's conscious in my mind in French, but not in English.

Interviewer But the reality is.

René   That I do them both.

He stopped and gazed into the air. A brief silence followed as I tried to grasp the meaning of what he had said, and presumably he did too. I broke the silence:

Interviewer That's interesting . . . So what you're saying is that it seems to be more intense in immersion because of the consciousness more than the actual reality of it? It's hard to know.

And he replied:

René   You see because I would do them both. And if I wasn't doing the immersion, I would probably do the same thing in

English anyway. So I would do it. It's just that in immersion, I'm conscious I'm doing it because I'm conscious of the fact that we're dealing in French.

I turned to subsequent interview questions, later asking him whether he thought the science curriculum lent itself to teaching language arts. René replied that it didn't because science was more important than language arts. He said that he could use science to promote language arts more, but that this would diminish the emphasis on science.

'Science could be more of a vehicle for language arts, but again, you can't have your cake and eat it too. If I chose to put more of my emphasis on language arts, then I would have to diminish the emphasis on science. To me science is the important thing.'

He went on to say that he saw secondary immersion as a maintenance program, where students could continue to use what they knew:

'To a certain extent, I see the immersion program at the high school level as more maintenance. In other words, science is a vehicle for them to use the things that they know, so that they will continue to use them.'

He also said that new learning took place in language arts classes, but that he did not take any special means to reinforce or build on this learning, echoing his previous point that putting more emphasis on language arts might diminish the emphasis on science:

'They also are learning things in their language arts classes, and I would hope that they would then choose to employ them for me. I demand that they write out full sentences whenever they do home-work, so I'm not going to let them get away with chicken scratches. They have to give me full sentences, so I would hope that they are using the tools that they have and the new tools they are acquiring for me, but I don't go to the specific length to ask them to do that. In other words, I would never have asked them to give me something that uses only the *passé composé*. I would never do that. You could, but I mean, it's an obvious trade-off. You up the language arts things; you're going to diminish the science.'

He said he felt that students were gaining new linguistic tools in their language arts and social studies classes, which were coordinated with one another, admitting that as a result he did not emphasize language as much.

'With the "sciences humaines" and the "français langue", they are getting new tools. The "sciences humaines" has its own curricular objectives, but it tends to be more verbal and written; and I know that he approaches it from a point of view where he is asked specifically to do those things, so I guess I allow myself to slide along and not put as much of an emphasis on that.'

René's reply to my question asking him what he thought language was perhaps gives us some clues as to why he may divorce himself somewhat from linguistic concerns. For him, language is first and foremost a means of thought and secondarily a means of communication:

Interviewer Most people do not like to answer this type of question.

René Oh, I love it.

Interviewer Obviously because this is the first time I've asked anybody what language is.

René What is language? OK, I have sort of two answers to what language is. Language is a means of thought. Most people start with language being a means of communication, and I don't think it starts there. I think it starts with the means of thought. Language determines the cubbyholes that will go into the mind. Language is a series of connections in the mind. It determines how the mind will work . . . So language is a means, is not a means, is the manner in which the mind is organized. People that speak the same language organize their minds in essentially similar ways. They then use that organization, and it has a verbal component, and then they communicate with it. It's perfectly possible to communicate without using verbal language.

Summary of case 4

René's class was mainly a teacher-directed class, in which the teacher used the Socratic method of question and answer to get students to think about their experiments and relate the ideas and concepts in the chapter being reviewed. The class was quite stimulating because of the teacher's energetic questioning and extensive probing for students' understandings. Clarity of language and explanation gave students good language models, and requiring students to verbalize their understandings of the material gave them some opportunity to use language, although most of the discourse was in short phrases or sentences.

The interview data suggest that René put most emphasis on active mental engagement of students in building scientific understanding. His description of the class I had seen was quite congruent with my observations. René loved everything about science, expressed a keen interest in scientific issues, and told me that he introduced discussion about these in class.

In contrast with Jean Jacques, a teacher in the elementary grades, who talked enthusiastically about 'training' students to 'acquire' their second language, René talked of the importance of preserving the science content of the lesson and mentioned the trade-offs one would have to make if one focused on language. He saw science as a way for students to maintain their linguistic skills, with new language learning taking place primarily in other subjects such as language arts and social studies, which he described as more verbal and written than was science. In talking about what language was, he said that he ascribed more importance to language as a means of thought than as a means of communication, perhaps suggesting why linguistic concerns may have been less of a priority for him.

René said that he used a few strategies in immersion classrooms that he did not in English. These were giving immersion students the English equivalent of science terms so that they 'could cross-reference their minds' and ensuring their comprehension of basic concepts and terminology before introducing new concepts. In addition to correcting students' grammar and having them write in complete sentences, René mentioned that he introduced oral language activities to encourage students to speak French. In reflecting that he did the same kinds of activities in English classes as in French, he suddenly realized that he was conscious of the linguistic goals for these activities for his French classes, whereas this was not the case for his English classes.

A silence followed when René came to this realization. I wonder what he thought in that brief moment of silence. I also wonder what immersion teachers think. How different is immersion teaching from teaching in first language programs? In Calvé's words: What are the distinguishing pedagogic traits of immersion? How does the teacher take into account the fact that he or she is teaching students a subject in their second language, in terms of linguistic and communicative strategies and methodological procedures? In other words, what really goes on in immersion classrooms?

'Quels sont les traits distinctifs de l'immersion sur le plan *pédagogique*? Comment l'enseignant tient-il compte du fait qu'il enseigne une matière dans la langue seconde de ses étudiants, en termes de stratégies linguistiques, communicatives, de démarches méthodolo-giques...?... Autrement dit, que se passe-t-il vraiment dans une classe d'immersion?' (Calvé, 1988: 35)

Summary and Conclusions

In this chapter, I have used four case studies to describe and discuss various aspects of the topic of language and subject matter integration.

Case study data are by nature particularistic and generalizable only to the extent that readers find the accounts resonant with their own experiences. They are valuable in providing insights and understanding of a given phenomenon and as a heuristic for future research. In this section, I discuss the understandings that I think can be gained from the four case studies, using the following interrelated topics to frame the discussion: immersion research; immersion strategies; teachers' beliefs and practices.

Immersion research

⌐ Research on immersion emphasizes the importance of promoting the productive use of language in the classroom through greater use of group work and authentic activities (Swain, 1987) and activity-based learning (Genesee, 1987). Currrent perspectives on language and science pedagogy which emphasize the importance of discourse and the use of language as an instrument of learning and thinking strengthen this perspective and serve also as the basis for improving the language learning environment in immersion classes.⌐The case study of Claudette, whose classroom was established as a community of learners engaged in discourse about science, can be seen as an example of a language rich science classroom while that of Michel suggests limitations of more traditional pedagogy.

However, in line with recent proposals for improving language teaching in immersion (Snow et al., 1989), more formal planning may still be needed to maximize the potential of science for language learning. In the interview, René mentioned that he introduced activities in his science teaching to promote students' French and indicated that he used the same kind of activities in English classes, without thinking of their benefits for English language learning. This suggests, but does not necessarily indicate for René, that there may be some danger in being only more conscious of promoting language learning and not taking active steps for tailoring science teaching to the needs of immersion students.

In addition, René's case study suggests a teacher who may be separating himself somewhat from language teaching, as did subject matter teachers in the language across the curriculum movement (Bullock Committee, 1975; Corson, 1990). While his need to ensure content learning and recognition of the trade-offs involved is valid, ways of capitalizing on the potential of science classes for language learning still need to be explored. This is especially important in view of research showing that there are important differences in the kinds of language used in different school subjects (Crandall, 1987). As well, ways need to be found to avoid compartmentalization of grammar and to help students focus on form-meaning relationships, as suggested by Swain (1987). However, as I experienced in my observations, it is very difficult to focus one's attention on anything but meaning in teaching content. It would be most helpful to know what immersion teachers think about these questions.

Equally important to the question of planned language teaching are the many unplanned opportunities teachers can seize on to enhance language learning. Cazden (1992a) stresses the importance of active teachers and introduces the metaphor of 'instructional detours' to capture how they introduce both planned and unplanned language teaching in their class-rooms. Jean Jacques provides an example of a teacher who can glide into a succession of teaching interludes to the benefit of both science and language learning. His mini-lesson on the word *microscopique* shows him capitalizing on a teachable moment and creating an 'instructional detour' in which he created a symphony of language and science teaching, using contextualization, personalization, humor and playfulness to rapidly tie scientific and lexical awareness and knowledge together.

Jean Jacques is also an example of a teacher who had an ethos for actively promoting language learning in his classroom. His interview data suggest that he had an almost missionary belief in the importance of rule-learning ('You are making rules and laws just like the rules of knowledge'). This was coupled with a belief in the need for the learner to build rules from linguistic data, using their intuition to guide them ('And the more they read, they become more aware of the different tenses that are collected in their heads. Does it sound good to your ears? That usually makes the judgement'). And he saw his role as fostering both ('You have the language barrier there, and you have to train your kids in French immersion to acquire those words'). Although formal planning of language objectives may be needed to improve immersion teaching, as suggested by Snow *et al.*, it would also be helpful for immersion teachers to share, discuss, and build on the ethos they have developed for actively promoting language learning in their subject matter classrooms. This may help them probe their underlying beliefs (see section following) and uncover the strategies they use to attend to language in their subject matter classrooms.

Immersion strategies

Researchers observing immersion classrooms in Canada (Laplante, 1993; Tardif, 1991, 1994; Weber, 1991; Weber & Tardif, 1991) and elsewhere (Artigal, 1991; Salomone, 1992a, b; Snow, 1990) have begun to uncover some of the important characteristics of immersion pedagogy. In this study, I used global observations of classrooms and interviews with teachers to explore strategies used to foster language learning in science classes. The small number of observations made, their short-term nature, and their focus on one subject lifted out of the context of the whole curriculum severely limited the kind of information I could gain.

Because of the interrelationship between language and content, it was very difficult to isolate immersion strategies through classroom observations alone without a great deal of inferencing. Teachers' accounts in the interviews proved to be a rich source of information, particularly when understood within the context of classrooms I had observed. Some of the strategies which I thought might be used for language learning (e.g. gesturing in the case of René) were not used specifically for this and seemed to have more to do with individual characteristics of the teacher. Other strategies were quite subtle and complex. For example, Claudette's use of paraphrasing was not to provide a correct model of language, as I had assumed, but to provide students with a mirror they could use in checking their thoughts (i.e., to allow the child to negotiate meaning with him/herself) and at the same time to promote a general learning strategy or tool that could be used in understanding French.

Despite the difficulties, the case study material can be helpful to teachers in thinking about and exploring the strategies they use. For example, Jean Jacques' case study helps understand the enabling role of the immersion teacher in helping students learn and use the language while they teach subject matter. His patience in allowing students to 'dig in' and search for a word, allowing them to use English and let the French come later, and the mini-lesson in which he encouraged students to use their word analysis skills will indeed probably strike a familiar note to many immersion teachers. Perhaps his unique phrasing, 'I train them to acquire' could be used by teachers to think about some of the ways they approach language teaching in the classroom.

In my observations, I was impressed by the tone of playfulness and experimentation about language, whether it was René's good-natured reminder to one of his students' anglicisms (which was also observed to occur in reverse from students to teacher); Claudette's emphasis on the importance of students' 'playing with' words; or the punning about *microscopique* in Jean Jacques' class ('C'est si petit que tu dois avoir . . . microscope'). Because playing with language entails bringing forth language as the object of attention, perhaps the theme of 'playfulness' could be used by teachers to think about the kinds of things they do to promote language learning in the classroom, including but going well beyond the proverbial classroom language games. This is particularly important given research on the metalinguistic benefits of bilingualism (Cummins & Swain, 1986) and recent research suggesting that greater metaphorical abilities with language may be a long-term effect of participation in immersion programs (Neufeld, 1993). This is also important in view of recent work suggesting the benefits of talk about language in creating a climate of intimacy and social bonding and making the language classroom a special kind of community of learning (Kramsch & McConnell-Ginet, 1992).

I also noted that teachers exploited students' knowledge of their first language, English, as a resource in using French and promoted cross-lingual transfer, whether in the case of René who told immersion students key words and phrases in English because he wanted them 'to be able to cross-reference their minds'; or Claudette pointing out that the word for '*pore*' was the same in French and English; or Michel allowing students to use the English and trusting that the French would come later. Stern (1983) identifies the role of the first language in second language learning as one of the three central issues in language learning and teaching and describes the vivid debate which has taken place on this topic over the centuries. It is important to explore the perspectives immersion teachers bring to the topic, for they appear to be quite different from those represented in this debate. René's statement, for example, that he gave students key words and phrases in English because he wanted them 'to be able to cross-reference their minds' suggests that his concern is with language as a tool for learning and thinking – an important insight given that research on bilingualism is revealing the benefits of dual coding of languages to memory (Lambert, 1990).

This study was not designed to provide generalizable data nor to yield a catalogue of strategies used by immersion teachers. The descriptive information in the case studies can, however, provide a context for exploring the question of teacher strategies further. According to Donmoyer (1990), case studies enable us to have vicarious encounters and expand our range of experiences. When readers experience a case through another's 'eyes', their range of interpretation and hence generalization is expanded. Hopefully, some of the case material will accord with teachers' experiences such that it will lead them to continue to examine and articulate their own strategies and practices, thus lending catalytic validity to this study (Lather, 1991).

Teachers' beliefs and practices

Recent research, including that done in immersion classrooms (Laplante, 1996; Salomone, 1992a), emphasizes the importance of exploring teachers' views on learning and instruction as a basis for preparing teachers and effecting change in current practice (Breen, 1991; Clark, 1988; Cumming, 1989; Hollingsworth, 1989; Johnson, 1992; Richardson *et al.*, 1991). Fenstermacher (1979) and Pajares (1992) view teacher beliefs as the 'single most important construct in educational research' (Pajares, 1992: 329). The case study material illustrates how investigating teachers' beliefs in conjunction with their practices can enrich our understanding of the integration of language and subject matter teaching in French immersion programs. Contrasting case studies of Claudette and Michel revealed that there were underlying commonalities between each teacher's approaches and views of science and her approaches and views of language. These in turn appeared to be reflected in the ways the teacher integrated language and science teaching and thus determined the implicit language learning curriculum provided to students. Similar observations are made by Laplante (1996) in a more extensive study of grade 1 immersion teachers' beliefs and practices.

With respect to integration, the contrasting case study data suggest that the way teachers shape the curriculum of the science class will also shape the curriculum of the language class. In Claudette's case, explanation, justification, and speculation were an inherent part of learning about science, and students were being given increasing responsibility for their learning; out of these arose an implicit language curriculum, which included use of a range of language functions, conversational turn-taking, consideration of the points of view of others, and collaborative talk. In contrast, a different kind of language curriculum seemed to emerge out of Michel's class. While language was used for communication, it was used for communication mainly between the teacher and the students; and what the students said appeared to serve little purpose other than to introduce the textbook material that the teacher wanted to transmit. If there was a message about language in this class, it was that language was something that you did something to rather than something that you did something with or that language was an object to be found or corrected rather than an inherent part of the learning process.

The underlying commonalities between each teacher's approaches and views of science and her approaches and views of language emerged clearly with Claudette and Michel on the particular days of the observations, with the particular set of instruments used in the study (including the researcher observing, interviewing, and interacting with the data in the analysis). They might not emerge as clearly if the teachers had been observed at other times and/or studied in other ways. The commonalities were also clear in the case of Jean Jacques, though more complicated with

René. The commonalities should not be seen as a law which governs the activities of teachers in a simple way; the complexity of teacher decision-making and of their underlying belief systems (Shavelson & Stern, 1981) would make this unlikely. However, they can be seen as one of the many threads that teachers can look for as they seek to unravel the complicated web of language and content integration.

In a recent article on teacher beliefs, Pajares (1992) suggests qualitative research methodology as especially appropriate for studies of this topic and discusses research showing the importance of investigating congruence between beliefs and behaviors. The case study data in this chapter lend support to this work. The case study data also suggest that it will be important not to study teacher beliefs in the context of a particular subject alone. It will be important to explore more fully the relationships between teachers' beliefs about language, their beliefs about subject matter, and ultimately about learning, if we are to have an understanding of what shapes current practices in second language teaching.

In conjunction with this, it will be important to recognize the important role teachers can play as generators of research and/or active collaborators in the research process (Clandinin & Connelly, 1986; Cole, 1989; Cole & Knowles, 1993; Grossman, 1990; Nunan, 1990; Rudduck & Hopkins, 1985; Wells, 1994). In addition to helping overcome problems of representing teachers (Nespor & Barylske, 1991) and 'speaking for others' (Alcoff, 1991) and the inevitable dangers of imposing a researcher's theoretical understandings on teachers' beliefs such as arose in our university-based study, this acknowledges that practical and formal inquiry can work together to increase our understanding of teaching and learning (Richardson, 1994).

Notes

1. The Context for Science Study was conducted under the rubric of the provincial assessment of science discussed in Chapter 1. This assessment was unusual in that it included three research studies (i.e. classroom context for science learning; performance tasks; and socio-scientific issues) in addition to the traditional assessment of student outcomes (Bateson *et al.*, 1992b).
2. Only one of us (the book's first author) was principally involved in the data collection of immersion classrooms and the preparation of case studies; the personal 'I' used in the rest of this chapter refers to this person.

4 Current Issues for the Immersion Language Curriculum

Introduction

Because of disparities between the performance of immersion and native French-speaking students in writing and speaking, immersion educators increasingly recognize a need for more systematic planning for language development in immersion programs. In this chapter, we explore some of the questions that should be considered in addressing this need.

Literature Review

Research on the language learning outcomes of French immersion programs, summarized in Chapter 1, provides valuable diagnostic information which can be used as a basis for improving immersion students' competence in French. This is complemented by observational research undertaken to investigate the context and processes which contribute to students' language learning. Research in kindergarten and grade 1 classrooms summarized in the previous chapter is beginning to uncover a rich array of strategies used by teachers to facilitate students' comprehension and production and enable them to learn through their second language (Laplante, 1993; Netten & Spain, 1989; Tardif, 1991, 1994; Weber, 1991; Weber & Tardif, 1991).

⌐ In a study of immersion classrooms in the higher grades (grades 3 and 6) in Ontario, researchers found certain limitations in the language learning conditions of the immersion classrooms they observed (Swain & Carroll, 1987; Swain, 1987). Specifically, they found that students had limited opportunities to engage in extended discourse in French. They also observed that immersion teachers rarely focused students' attention on the relationship of form to meaning when they taught subject matter and provided unsystematic feedback to students about their linguistic errors. In addition, the language of the classroom was functionally restricted in some ways, with certain uses of the language (e.g. the conditional verb form, aspectual distinctions in past tenses) occurring infrequently in teachers' speech. Our case studies of grades 4, 7 and 10 science classrooms (Chapter 3) were undertaken with a different orientation than was the Swain & Carroll study, making comparisons difficult. However, we note informally that attention to form-meaning relationships and error feedback appeared to be infrequent but that there appeared to be a wider variation in the extent to which students were provided with opportunities to engage in extended discourse in French.]

The observational research on immersion classrooms provides a small empirical basis for exploring curricular and instructional questions related to the French language development of immersion students. It is joined by experimental studies designed specifically to address the question of how to improve immersion students' linguistic competence in French. The experimental studies are based on current second language curriculum theory, which seeks to combine less formal, experiential teaching, involving the natural, unanalyzed use of language, with more formal language teaching based on analysis and practice of the linguistic code (Allen, 1983; Stern, 1982, 1992). This approach, referred to as a functional-analytic approach, also finds support in the work of other researchers investigating the effects of instruction in communicative classroom settings (e.g. Lightbown & Spada, 1990; Spada & Lightbown, 1993; White, 1991).

A study by Harley (1987a, 1989), which was designed to teach grade 6 immersion students the distinction between the *imparfait* and the *passé composé*, showed only short-term and no long-term effects on immersion students' oral and written control of this distinction. Our study in Chapter 2, which was designed to teach the use of the conditional to grade 7 students, showed both short-term and long-term positive effects in writing and some gains in speaking. A study by Lyster (1994a), designed to teach grade 8 students sociolinguistic variation in the use of *tu* and *vous*, also showed improvement in students' speaking and writing both in the short-term and long-term.

Various differences in the studies, such as the design of the experimental materials, the age group of the students, and the linguistic features being taught, may have contributed to the different results, and the effectiveness of a functional-analytic approach to the teaching of language in immersion programs remains a question for continued research. Particularly problematic is the difficulty students have in attending to the form of language in freer, highly meaningful speaking tasks (the code-communication dilemma referred to by Stern, 1983). And as noted by Harley (1987b), the linguistic features selected by researchers on the basis of analyses of learner difficulties (i.e. their hypothesized needs) may not necessarily be perceived as vital for instruction or learning by participants in the experiment. Further information is needed not only on what works but what is feasible in the real life of the classroom so that we can gain a more complete understanding of language teaching in immersion.

In addition to the research reviewed above, specific proposals relating to the need to plan for language development have appeared in the literature. Concerned with the number of grammatical errors and their tendency to fossilize in students' speech, Lyster (1987) initially called for a language syllabus (or curriculum) based on students' errors to be introduced in immersion beginning in the early grades. In a later refinement of this proposal (1990), he discusses more thoroughly the content of his proposed language syllabus. According to Lyster, this content is to be determined by the language functions learners are expected to perform, the language structures needed to express these functions, and those which recur in the learner's interlanguage (i.e. the difficulties of immersion students).

⌐ In order to maximize the language learning potential of immersion programs, Snow et al. (1989) recommend that immersion teachers systematically incorporate (and plan for) language objectives when they teach subject matter. They provide a conceptual framework for integrating language and content instruction, and they suggest that objectives be derived from both the language and the academic curriculum, as well as from assessment and ongoing evaluation of learners' academic and communicative needs and of their developing language skills. In addition, they propose that immersion teachers deal with two kinds of second language objectives when they teach subject matter or content: (a) content *obligatory* language objectives, which specify the language students need to develop, master and communicate about a given content material and include both structural and functional aspects of language; and (b) content *compatible* language objectives, which are compatible with the concept or information to be taught but are not required for successful content mastery.⌐

Lyster's proposal for a language curriculum and Snow et al.'s proposal for integrating subject matter with language teaching objectives are not mutually exclusive, and they are consistent with a consensus among immersion educators that immersion students' speech can be improved in two ways: (1) by strengthening the communicative, experiential aspects of the immersion approach by providing students with opportunities to interact in French and write and speak the language; and (2) by complementing the communicative, experiential approach with more explicit and systematic attention to language teaching. The need to pay more explicit attention to language teaching represents a challenge to immersion practitioners and raises interesting questions for consideration in planning a language curriculum for immersion programs.

Questions for Consideration

Meeting the program's dual goals

A first consideration would be the goals of the immersion program, which include both communicative proficiency in the second language and learning of the subject matter of the regular school curriculum. Any proposal should be designed so that the two goals of language and subject matter teaching can be served with maximum efficiency. The proposals of both Lyster and of Snow *et al.* consider the communicative functions needed by students to learn subject matter as one of the bases for deriving objectives and therefore address the efficiency question. However, Lyster's proposal for a language curriculum (or syllabus) carries with it the danger of rigidity and over specificity with respect to selection of objectives and may constrain the language curriculum unnecessarily. In addition, the prespecification of functions and structures suggested in the proposal is not consistent with the dynamic approach to language teaching underlying the immersion approach; and it directs our energies to developing lists or inventories of what is to be learned, without considering how these may be integrated into subject matter teaching.

Snow *et al.*'s proposal for more systematic planning provides a framework for immersion teachers to work in their role as language and subject matter teachers and allows considerable flexibility in the specification of objectives. A dynamic view is presented of the immersion teacher as a person who actively diagnoses students' language needs, noting aspects of language development that require clarification or extended practice. The proposal has the suppleness that is needed in the immersion classroom, where teachers must not only plan but also be alert to the many opportunities for language teaching that occur during the day so that they can quickly and spontaneously incorporate these into their teaching. As we found in Chapter 3, the case study of one teacher (René) suggests a teacher who may be separating himself somewhat from language teaching, as did subject matter teachers in the language across the curriculum movement

(Bullock Committee, 1975). The case study also suggests that there may be some danger in being only more conscious of promoting language learning and not taking active steps for tailoring subject matter teaching to the needs of immersion students. The Snow *et al.* proposal leads more naturally (although not necessarily) to considering how we can strengthen the links between language and subject matter teaching so that they can mutually support one another. This is especially important in view of research showing that there are important differences in the kinds of language used in different school subjects (Crandall, 1987) and has yet to be addressed in a systematic way for immersion, as it has been, for example, in other kinds of language teaching programs (Mohan, 1986; Strevens, 1977).

However, although formal planning of language objectives may be needed to improve immersion teaching, it will also be helpful for immersion teachers to share, discuss, and build on the ethos they have developed for actively promoting language learning in their subject matter classrooms. As discussed in Chapter 3, this may help them probe the beliefs underlying their practices and uncover the strategies they use to attend to language in their subject matter classrooms. The case study of Jean Jacques in Chapter 3 is an example of a teacher who actively promotes language learning by 'training students to acquire'. A further useful example can be found in Lyster's (1994b) description of a classroom in which teacher and students 'negotiatied form' as well as meaning.

Weighing the importance of language teaching in immersion

A further consideration in the call for planning a language curriculum relates to determining the relative importance of language teaching in the whole school curriculum. Ultimately, how this is addressed brings us to fundamental questions regarding the degree and kinds of bilingualism we want students to attain in immersion programs and the yardstick we might use to measure this. This can only be understood in relation to the sociocultural goals of the program. Like other kinds of French programs, French immersion is supported through the Federal Government's bilingual education policy, the goal of which is to bring together the French and English solitudes in Canada. As Stern points out:

> Bilingualism, in this situation, although also of personal value to the individual, is mainly introduced as a social good to be developed through schooling because of its importance as a binding force in the society across its linguistic divisions. (Stern, 1983: 437)

Because of the sociocultural goals, functional bilingual skills are seen by many as the most important objective for language learning in immersion.

However, functional bilingualism is a vague and relative notion and can mean anything from the ability to understand and make oneself understood and get by in everyday social situations to the ability to function like a well-educated native-speaker in demanding social and professional settings (Calvé, 1988; Savignon, 1983). This makes the expected degree of proficiency a matter of interpretation and brings with it a host of difficult questions relating to who, when, and how we should evaluate or judge that proficiency. These questions have no easy answers, but they need to be discussed in weighing the relative importance of the language curriculum in immersion.

This is not to deny that we should strive to improve students' spoken and written language, and in particular to promote linguistic accuracy. The importance of linguistic accuracy to the comprehensibility of a message is widely recognized in language teaching and constitutes a valid educational argument for improving immersion students' speech. However, contextual factors and the collaborative nature of communication are also important factors in comprehensibility, suggesting that we need to keep the matter in perspective (Savignon, 1983).

There are also other valid educational arguments for promoting accuracy. Lyster (1990) points out that language can reflect cultural values and viewpoints, and should be seen not only as a functional code but as a means of discovering the richness of difference transmitted through language and found in other cultures. Calvé (1988) reminds us that there are important educational dimensions to learning a second language, which should not be overshadowed by the functional goals of the program. He distinguishes between two kinds of objectives for language programs, which he views as complementing one another: (a) those related to linguistic *training* and the development of functional bilingual skills (basic functional skills in comprehension and written and oral expression); and (b) those related to a linguistic *education* (i.e. knowledge of the internal structure of the language, comprehension and appreciation of its culture and literature and of the variety of registers of language, developing a taste for nuance and precision in language use, and the desire for continued growth in all of these aspects). These educational arguments are good reasons for placing more emphasis on improving immersion students' written and spoken language. They are also joined by another reasonable justification, which is that any educational program should strive to maximize its benefits to students.

Among the primary goals of French immersion are to enable students to become proficient in French and to increase their appreciation and understanding of francophone cultures. It will be important to weigh the balance between instrumental and educational goals (i.e. in Calvé's terms, between linguistic training and a linguistic education). To what extent we should be creating our own linguistic and cultural norms when the objective is to understand the linguistic and cultural norms of another group is an interesting question for immersion education.

Maintaining a balanced view of communicative proficiency

A third important consideration in discussing the language curriculum for immersion relates to the multi-faceted nature of communicative proficiency. Canale & Swain (1980) hypothesize four components of communicative competence: grammatical competence, which includes knowledge of vocabulary, word formation, pronunciation, spelling, and sentence formation; discourse competence, which includes the ability to arrange ideas in logical sequence and organize meanings effectively; sociolinguistic competence, which refers to the ability to use the appropriate style of speech; and strategic competence, which refers to the ability to overcome communication difficulties and maintain the flow of communication. Other theorists also propose social and sociocultural competences as important dimensions (Corson, 1990). When considering the kind of language planning to undertake in immersion programs, it is important to go beyond grammatical competence alone and to include all aspects of communicative competence.

In the past, the performance of native French-speaking students has served as an important benchmark for evaluating the communicative skills of French immersion students. Because of this, linguistic differences between immersion and French-speaking students have been overemphasized, and there has been an implicit message that those areas which are not comparable to native-speakers (i.e. grammatical and sociolinguistic competence) deserve more attention than those which are (i.e. discourse and strategic competence). However, it is important to remember that research results are based on group averages, aimed at overall evaluation of student outcomes. While they provide useful diagnostic information for program improvement, they form only a part of the information that should be used in instructional decision-making.

In teaching, we need to examine the actual performance levels of immersion students in all areas of communicative competence. Otherwise, we may skew the curriculum in favor of those areas found deficient and overlook other important areas, particularly those not measured or attended to in research. We may also fail to consider the need for instruction which attends to the full range of student abilities found on the measures used to evaluate students' French language skills. In addition, we should question whether we should base the standards of performance of immersion students on any outside group rather than on criteria developed within the program, for it is quite possible that we may want to have different standards in certain areas of communicative competence than those attained by native-speakers of the language.

Attending to the implicit language curriculum

In planning for language development in immersion, it will be useful to view the immersion program as having two kinds of language curricula: one a more explicit curriculum, which is planned according to the criteria suggested in the proposals discussed previously or according to other criteria, and the other an implicit curriculum, which is largely unplanned and somewhat incidental. Genesee defines the latter as 'embedded in the academic content and materials of the program of study and in the ways in which teachers use instructional materials to teach academic content' (Genesee, 1989: 19).

The instructional approach used to teach subject matter can restrict or enlarge the communication requirements in the classroom and thereby influence the implicit curriculum and ultimately what is learned. Recent work in English as a second language shows that different functional purposes stimulate different types of language and discourse patterns (Nunan, 1991). More broadly, we suggest that the communicative skills needed for learning subject matter in classrooms with a more interactionist or a constructivist approach to teaching are greater than those in classrooms with a more traditional, didactic approach in which the teacher does most of the talking and there is little interaction among students. This is because the former kinds of classrooms aim at understanding and place considerably more emphasis on the use of language as a tool for learning and on the socially constructed nature of knowledge. Consider the following description of a science classroom from this perspective, for example:

All too often the discussion between pupils in science classrooms is confined to administrative details, such as who will go and get the equipment, where graph paper is, who will measure the time, and so on. All too rarely do we find pupils talking about their own conceptualisations of the scientific ideas underlying the 'scientific' activity they are meant to be engaged upon. Also, in our opinion, if learners are to change their views, or to appreciate what is being taught, it is important that they are clear about their *own* views. (Osborne & Freyberg, 1985: 37)

In our study of language and science teaching discussed in the previous chapter, two contrasting science classrooms were observed and described. One classroom was set up like a communicative arena, in which all shared their knowledge and developed their understandings. The teacher encouraged students to speculate about science and be comfortable with the view that there might be 'no right answer' to some questions. Students questioned one another and discussed their viewpoints; they had many opportunities to use French productively and they used a wide variety of language functions and structures. Explanation, justification, and speculation were an inherent part of learning about science. Out of this arose an implicit language curriculum, which included use of a range of language functions, conversational turn-taking, consideration of the points of view of others, and collaborative talk.

In contrast, in the second classroom, a didactic approach to teaching science prevailed. Students' language consisted of mainly a word, phrase or sentence, given in response to the teacher's questions. While language was used for communication, it was used for communication mainly between teacher and students. There was little elaboration or expansion of language and little interaction among students. The teacher of this classroom used some specific strategies directed at promoting students' language learning; however, these were of a rather minor sort involving technical skills and appeared to be arbitrary insertions rather than arising inherently out of the teaching of the subject matter. The message in this class was that language was an object to be found or corrected rather than an inherent part of the learning process.

If teachers derive their objectives from the needs of learning subject matter and an ongoing assessment of students' demonstrated language proficiency or lack thereof in meeting the academic demands of the subject matter classroom, it will be necessary to consider also how we should strengthen the implicit curriculum, which is influenced by how teachers teach subject matter. We should recognize more fully that quite different areas of need might arise in different classrooms – language functions which will determine the syntax being used, logical connectors needed to express higher level thought, and interrelation of everyday language and scientific language which may shape the vocabulary used in the classroom.

In his work on the importance of talk in teaching and learning, Wells (1991) analyzes the conversational interaction patterns of a discussion in science and shows how the context of preceding talk influenced what followed by providing students with a 'pool of words and phrases' that they could draw on in ensuing conversational turns. He also shows how the teacher moved between everyday discourse and the technical discourse of science, creating a bridge between the two for the students and giving them the opportunity to appropriate and internalize a 'cultural tool' so that in the future they would be able to use it on their own (Wells, 1991: 17). The cultural tools Wells refers to are the more formal ways of conceptualization found in scientific discourse. We should not overlook the importance of these procedures of appropriation and internalization for grammatical learning, while at the same time keeping in mind Swain's (1985) hypothesis that students may need to be pushed to make the link between form and meaning. Research on the importance of talk and more broadly on the social foundations of learning (Cazden, 1992b) will be critical in helping us gain a deeper understanding of how best to promote the linguistic development of immersion students.

Keeping in mind the social/psychological nature of language learning

The above discussion brings us to a final consideration relating to the social and psychological aspects of language learning. Immersion children form a speech community in the classroom where they are successful in communicating with one another and with the teacher. It is widely recognized that the success and confidence they have in communicating what they want to say and their lack of contact with francophone peers gives them no strong social incentive to develop further toward native-speaker norms. In an interview of secondary immersion students conducted as part of the study in Chapter 3, students said that they did not find their French class useful because they learned about verbs, in particular the subjunctive; and they said that this verb form wasn't really used or needed except if one wanted to be president (in their words, 'tu ne parles pas avec le subjonctif; seulement si tu veux être président ou quelque chose').[1] Yet, there were many occasions in our conversation in which the subjunctive was called for. The value of linguistic accuracy is indeed remote to these students, as is the idealized native-speaker norm that they are expected to strive towards.

In addition, other social factors are operating. Research on language learning from a sociocultural perspective shows that bilingual individuals or groups (e.g. those forming learning communities) often construct a 'variation space' which is different from that of native-speakers in order to maintain identity or exhibit status (Romaine, 1982; Savignon, 1991). In the following interchange from a grade 7 classroom (personal observation), two students are chatting with one another during a writing activity, and one student asks the other for an eraser (*une efface*). In chatting they use an extreme form of anglicized French, different from their classroom French:

Child 1   Guess quel time j'ai allé au bed. J'ai allé au bed à midnight
                 . . . Est-ce que je peux avoir ton efface?

Child 2   Quelqu'un a stealé le; quelqu'un a rip off mon efface.

When we casually ask Child 2 what he said ('Comment? Je n'ai pas entendu. Quelqu'un a?'), he answers that what he said was not French, but slang ('Ça c'est pas le français; c'est le slang'). He then pauses, and says: 'Quelqu'un a volé mon efface', at the same time waving his hands as if he were flying and thus playing on the dual meaning of the verb *voler*, to fly and to steal.

As this incident shows, children have considerable sophistication in the use of language, switching from their classroom French (sometimes characterized as an interlanguage) to their own 'slang' and back again according to the interlocutor. If they can move from a classroom register to a more personal one, they also have the potential to move to a more correct register of French when they perceive it desirable or necessary. As educators, it is our task to give students the underlying knowledge which will enable them to do this when the social conditions and motivation are present. This requires that we view the French language skills students acquire in immersion programs as a basis that can be maintained and developed throughout their lives rather than as an endpoint. This does not mean that we should reject grammatical teaching. But we must pay more attention to how it is taught (Celce-Murcia, 1991). Helping students see that grammar is a resource to be used in the comprehension and creation of their own spoken and written language and developing their intrinsic motivation to improve may help resolve any apparent conflict between the educational and instrumental goals of second language learning.

In this regard, further development and experimentation with pedagogic materials based on a functional-analytic approach to language teaching should be pursued, particularly in those areas where the functional richness of grammar can be explored (e.g. the verb system that has been found to be a major area of difficulty for immersion children, see Harley, 1993). As suggested in Chapter 2, providing a systematic grammatical focus, creating an interactive and motivating learning environment, and stimulating students' metalinguistic awareness should be critical elements in designing such materials.

Summary and Conclusions

In recent years, there has been growing recognition among immersion educators that more systematic planning for the immersion language curriculum is needed to improve students' competence in French. In this chapter, we set forth some of the questions that should be considered in addressing this need. An important consideration in our planning is efficiency and effectiveness with respect to meeting the goals of the program, which include both communicative proficiency in the second language and learning of the subject matter of the regular school curriculum. While determining what we should teach is necessary to planning, developing inventories or lists of what is to be learned has only limited value unless we also work towards strengthening the links between language and subject matter teaching so that they can mutually support one another. A more dynamic and fluid approach to language planning such as that contained in the framework proposed by Snow *et al.* (1989) is a good first step in this direction. However, perhaps attention might also be given to developing a framework which will integrate language and subject matter teaching, such as has been attempted for English second language education.

A second consideration in planning for language development in immersion relates to discussing and clarifying why we want students to gain proficiency in the second language, what degree of proficiency we aim for, and what yardstick we might use to measure this. Vagueness in the goal of functional proficiency has allowed us to avoid these questions; but the call for more systematic language planning obliges us to consider these more carefully. In addition, it will be important to weigh the balance between instrumental and educational goals in learning a second language (i.e. in Calvé's terms, between linguistic training and a linguistic education). To what extent we should be creating our own linguistic and cultural norms when the objective is to understand the linguistic and cultural norms of another group is an interesting question for immersion education.

In planning the language curriculum, we need also to keep in mind that communicative competence in a second language involves a number of dimensions including grammatical, sociolinguistic, discourse, and strategic competences. Research and evaluation studies of immersion programs provide us with a large body of useful diagnostic information on the language skills of immersion students but tend to overemphasize linguistic differences between immersion and French-speaking students. Thus, there has been an implicit message that those areas of communicative competence which are not comparable to native-speakers deserve more attention than those which are. Decision-making in the classroom should centre around the instructional value of all aspects of communicative competence and should consider the progress of all children. We might also question whether we should base the standards of performance of immersion students on any outside group rather than on criteria developed within the program, for it is quite possible that we may want to have different standards in certain areas of communicative competence than those attained by native-speakers of the language.

Another consideration in planning for language development in immersion relates to the contribution made by the implicit language curriculum to the kind of language children learn. The instructional approach used to teach subject matter can restrict or enlarge the communication requirements in the classroom and therefore influence the implicit language curriculum. We should recognize more fully that quite different areas of need might arise in different classrooms; for example, language functions which will determine the syntax being used, logical connectors needed to express higher level thought, and the interrelation of everyday language and scientific language which may shape the vocabulary and structures used in the classroom. If language objectives are derived from an assessment of learners' academic and communicative needs in learning subject matter, we should attend to the factors which shape these needs and therefore work toward strengthening not only the explicit but the implicit language curriculum. In addition, we should carefully consider recent research on the importance of talk and the social foundations of learning, for this may provide us with a deeper understanding of how best to promote the linguistic development of immersion students.

A final consideration in planning a language curriculum for immersion relates to the psychological and social aspects of language learning. Identification and motivation are powerful factors in determining what and how much is learned (Savignon, 1991; Snow, 1992). We should view the French language skills students acquire in immersion programs as a basis that can be maintained and developed throughout their lives rather than as an endpoint. This does not mean that we should reject grammatical teaching. Helping students see that grammar is a resource to be used in creating meaning and developing their intrinsic motivation to improve their spoken and written language may help resolve any apparent conflict between the educational and instrumental goals of second language learning.

Recent calls for more systematic planning for the immersion language curriculum present a challenge to immersion educators. Concrete proposals for action are helpful, but more thoughtful examination of the questions involved is also necessary. Hopefully, this chapter can spark some discussion, particularly at the interface of researchers with practioners, where unique answers to the question of language planning in immersion may be found.

Notes

1. The irony of these Canadian students using the word *président* instead of *premier ministre* should not be lost on the reader.

5 French Immersion Teacher Education: A Study of Two Programs[1]

Introduction

The dramatic growth of French immersion in Canada brought with it an unprecedented demand for qualified teaching personnel and specialized teacher preparation programs. Canadian universities began to respond to this situation in the late 1970s and 1980s when the demand for qualified teachers became acute. In a survey of universities conducted for the Canadian Association of Immersion Teachers, Frisson-Rickson & Rebuffot (1986) found that there were a growing number of pre-service courses related to immersion but relatively few comprehensive programs for preparing immersion teachers. While this report provided useful descriptive information, it was not designed to probe the theoretical framework of existing programs, their clientele, and participants' experiences. Information of this nature is needed to inform the development and expansion of specialized teacher education programs in French immersion. The need for a base of more valid information about courses and programs to inform policymakers and educators in teacher education is echoed by other researchers (Goodlad, 1991; Howey & Zimpher, 1989).

To address the need for more systematic research information to guide the development of immersion teacher education, we conducted case studies of immersion teacher education in two institutions in Western Canada. Our studies focused on the clientele for these programs, the models on which the programs are based, participants' experiences and needs, and future educational planning; and we analyzed our findings in relation to research on teacher education. In this chapter, we provide descriptive summaries of the two programs and discuss our conclusions.

Literature Review

Many educators have signalled the need for specialized immersion teacher preparation and have identified its key components (Bernhardt & Schrier, 1992; Calvé, 1989; Frisson-Rickson & Rebuffot, 1986; Hébert, 1987; Obadia, 1984; Tardif, 1985). Some of the components, such as general professional training (i.e. foundations for teaching), subject matter knowledge, and the practicum are those that would be found generally in all teacher education programs. Other components, such as linguistic competence, language and culture, theories of second language learning, and French second language and immersion teaching methodology, are the distinctive building blocks needed to develop immersion teacher education from theoretical, linguistic and cultural, and pedagogical perspectives.

While there is general agreement on the knowledge and experience required of immersion teachers, more information is needed on how current programs and offerings meet the components for effective immersion teacher education we find in the literature (see Hébert, 1987; Majhanovich & Fish, 1988; Majhanovich & Gray, 1992). In addition, it is important that further work in immersion teacher education relate to issues and theoretical developments in the broader field of teacher education so that the programs are not developed in isolation (Lapkin et al., 1990).

Major investigations advocating reform in teacher education have recently been conducted (BC Royal Commission, 1988; Carnegie Forum on Education, 1986; Channon, 1971; Holmes Group, 1986, 1990; the National Commission, 1985; Ontario Royal Commission, 1995). In addition, recent research yields a rich body of descriptive information on teacher education programs in the United States. Howey & Zimpher (1989), for example, conducted case studies of six exemplary teacher education programs and identified several of their key characteristics, such as a clear conception of teaching/schooling, program coherence, curriculum articulation, faculty collegiality, and the use of student cohorts. In addition, Goodlad's team of researchers (Goodlad, 1991; Goodlad et al., 1990) conducted case studies of 29 programs, using a set of expectations or essential presuppositions about teacher education to guide their examination. Among these are a clear sense of mission, institutional commitment and support, carefully selected and guided classes of students, coherent programs, an adequate supply of exemplary clinical settings, modeling of teaching practices and conditions, and critical inquiry into the nature of teaching and schooling.

These researchers provide a valuable set of parameters and principles for examining current programs. Work clarifying and categorizing major conceptual orientations guiding the development of teacher education programs is also important. According to Feiman-Nemser (1989), there are five basic conceptual orientations: the academic, the practical, the technical, the personal, and the critical/social. These do not serve as equally valid alternatives from which to choose but rather provide a source of ideas and practices to draw on in establishing programs. As she notes, a conceptual framework identifying the major tasks that should be addressed by pre-service teacher preparation programs, regardless of their orientation, is still needed to provide guidance for program development and evaluation.

In addition to understanding different conceptual orientations underlying teacher preparation, it is important to gain familiarity with various important perspectives in current research on teacher education, such as the development of a knowledge base about teaching; the growing importance of inquiry/reflective models of teacher preparation; the relationship between theory and practice; the view of learning to teach and teaching as a continuum; and the need for collaboration among various constituents in delivering teacher education programs (Lapkin *et al.*, 1990).

Methodology

Our case studies of immersion teacher education programs were conducted in 1989-90 in two institutions in Western Canada, one an anglophone institution (Simon Fraser University) and the other a francophone institution (Faculté Saint-Jean). We selected the institutions from the four programs in Western Canada which, according to Frisson-Rickson & Rebuffot (1986), offered an immersion teacher education program.[2]

We examined the programs in relation to theoretical perspectives on teacher education and immersion education. Consistent with research on teacher education programs (Howey & Zimpher, 1989; National Center for Research on Teacher Education, 1988; Sirotnik, 1989), we attempted to examine important program level dimensions (e.g. program structure, underlying philosophy, coherence, and ethos); investigate the nature of the curricular experiences offered, including their organization, content and rationale; and gain background information on participants, determine their relationships, and access their perspectives in a variety of areas.

We used methodologies arising from naturalistic inquiry and responsive case studies (Guba & Lincoln, 1981; Lincoln & Guba, 1985; Stake, 1978) to examine the programs in depth. This included: (a) interviews of participants (i.e. university administrators and faculty, instructors, students, and cooperating teachers); (b) participant observation of courses, seminars, and practica; and (c) content analyses of program and course materials and institutional policy documents. Participant observation included extensive site visits (15 days at the Faculté Saint-Jean and 12 days at Simon Fraser University), during which we conducted interviews, had informal discussions and encounters with participants, and observed university coursework and practicum experiences. In order to strengthen cross-site comparisons and overcome a possible bias arising from the fact that we were based at one of the institutions being studied (Simon Fraser University), we invited one member from each site to collaborate with us in collecting the data at the other site.

We collected a variety of data requiring different procedures for analysis. We examined policy documents and interview transcriptions through the use of content analyses, using qualitative data analysis procedures as advocated by Miles & Huberman (1984). To best reflect the available data, triangulation was used where possible. In this study, three categories of data were analyzed in such a way that each acted as a check on the other: 1) institutional program materials and policy documents; (2) interviews and observations; and (3) literature on teacher education and immersion education.

We kept field journals containing all notes and comments on our experiences, and taped and later transcribed interviews. After each day's visit, we reviewed notes, compared reactions, and discussed findings, interpretations and further questions to be addressed. We then prepared a written summary based on the notes and findings. The summaries, field journals, transcribed interviews, and program documents formed the data set. We analyzed the data from one site visit to the next and used the analyses to guide subsequent visits in order to verify or obtain additional information and explore inconsistencies. As the study progressed, we isolated major themes and developed categories to organize the data. We refined these through a constant sifting through the data and through information obtained in subsequent visits. We then developed a case study outline and prepared a draft case study report. After submitting the draft for member checks, we prepared the final report. Our final report (Day & Shapson, 1991) contains the full case study accounts upon which we have based the descriptive summaries which follow.

Case Study Results

Faculté Saint-Jean

Faculté Saint-Jean, a French language faculty of the University of Alberta, Edmonton, serves students capable of pursuing university studies in French. Its mission is to serve the needs of francophones in Western

Canada, contribute to the cultural enrichment of its students and of Albertan life in general, and foster French culture in Western Canada. Nestled in a small francophone community, it is a focal point and centre of cultural life for franco-Albertans, many of whom have settled around the campus.

From its beginnings as a religious institution to its present day faculty status, Saint-Jean carries with it a history of struggle and determination for the survival of a linguistic minority. Those responsible for preparing future teachers have been active agents in the development of their institution, remain committed to its mission, and are active in franco-Albertan community life. Some of them are also its graduates and former teachers, and they carry with them the humanistic traditions of the classical *collège* in which they studied and taught.

Students preparing to become teachers at Saint-Jean bring with them their own histories and diverse backgrounds and thus also contribute to the context in which they will learn to become teachers. Some students, although only a small number, are franco-Albertans, a few telling us that they had come to regain a language they had almost lost. In the words of one student:

'Je suis francophone et j'avais perdu ma langue presque complètement. Quand j'ai décidé de retourner aux études, je voulais le faire en français. Alors je me suis lancée ici.'

Others are francophones from various Canadian provinces in which French speakers are a minority (e.g. New Brunswick) or a majority (Québec). They are joined by students from various French-speaking countries (France, Vietnam, countries of the Middle East and Africa) and by a growing number of anglophone students.

The cosmopolitan student body contributes both to the richness and to the complexity of Saint-Jean, which must remain faithful to its original mission of meeting the special needs of franco-Albertans and at the same time provide post-secondary studies in French to all qualified students. This institutional complexity embodies an essential reality about language, which is its intimate connection to the sociocultural context, and this lesson is not lost on students as they learn that their own linguistic and cultural experience may not be the same as that of their classmates.

The sociocultural context in which students complete their studies is an important part of the lived experience of Saint-Jean and forms part of its dynamism, but other aspects are equally important in understanding the nature of the Saint-Jean experience. These are the small size of the institution, its warm and familial environment, and the close collegial relationships among students and faculty.

United by common experiences and goals, the faculty worked together as a team to develop the teacher education program in the late 1970s and to respond to the growing demand for French immersion teachers that was beginning to become apparent at that time. The philosophy of education underlying the program expresses their collective views on the nature of the learner, the teacher, and the human being. A synthesis is included in the syllabi of all courses and discussed with students at the beginning of each course so that students can react to and share in it and use it as a basis for developing their own personal philosophy.

One does not have to be at Saint-Jean for long to see that the philosophy arises out of deep beliefs and is enacted by the individuals who contributed to its development. Many strands are woven through the program and form part of the Saint-Jean experience: personal development and fulfillment, social responsibility, critical inquiry and reflection, a discovery-oriented pedagogy, and creativity. Faculty are very conscious that they are transmitting values, see themselves as important role models for students, and live and practice what they teach. As one faculty member told us:

'I think that we feel that we want to transmit certain values that are important, that it is not only knowledge per se. The person of the teacher we feel needs to be educated as well.'

This is done in multiple ways: through the social engagement of some of the faculty members and their involvement in minority language issues and community activities; through the relationships they have with their students and the intellectual and affective climate for learning they create; and through their professional engagement and teamwork which have developed, nurtured, and sustained the teacher education program.

An important cornerstone of the Saint-Jean program is a commitment to preparing teachers capable of working in an immersion or a francophone setting. To this end, the program offers a set of professional courses designed to enable the future teacher to gain knowledge about teaching, the learner, and the domain of French immersion and minority language education and to develop linguistic skills and professional skills and attitudes. All students at Saint-Jean are required to take a core of courses in French language, linguistics, and French-Canadian civilization and culture. They also do all their coursework in French and thus are provided with a rich context in which to further develop their linguistic skills.

Education students are required to take Methods courses in lesson and unit planning and in teaching French, reading, mathematics, and social studies in a French immersion or minority language setting. In addition, they take required foundational courses in Child or Adolescent Psychology, Interpersonal Communication, the History of Canadian Education, and Educational Administration and Media. Although the research literature indicates that foundational courses are frequently criticized by student teachers (Book et al., 1983; Wideen & Holborn, 1986), Saint-Jean student teachers appear to recognize and accept their importance. Perhaps this is because these courses are used to address students' personal beliefs about teaching or because the sociocultural context provides a dimension of relevance and meaning to many of the issues explored in the courses.

In addition to their required coursework, students take a practicum program which is organized into three phases and designed to allow students to have early opportunities to explore whether they want to become teachers, a gradual induction into teaching, and a range of experiences in the schools. The first phase is campus-based with some observation in the schools and is taken by undergraduates in their second year and by after-degree candidates in their first. The second and third phases include 13 weeks of field experience and are taken in the final year, which is a year of professional training integrating course and field work (see Table 5.1). This Professional Year gives students the opportunity to experience interaction between theory and practice and provides a means of professional socialization, both considered to be essential features in effective teacher education (see, for example, Goodlad, 1991; Howey & Zimpher, 1989; Tom, 1991). Reflection, self-evaluation, and personal development are encouraged through a variety of program dimensions, including logs, journals, philosophy statements, research projects, a contract system, and developmental supervision. Cooperative work and collegial sharing are also encouraged.

Table 5.1 Faculté Saint-Jean: The professional year

Semester 1		Semester 2	
7 weeks	*6 weeks*	*4 weeks*	*9 weeks*
3 half courses in Curriculum and Methodology	Phase II: 4 weeks in the schools/2 weeks on campus	One half-course of the student's choice in Education and 1 half-course in Ed. Psych.	Phase III: 9 weeks of student teaching

The extended nine-week practicum, which comes at the end of the students' final professional year, is seen as indispensable to completing one's preparation for teaching. The problems with extended field experiences (e.g. wide diversity in cooperating teachers; students socialized into the norms of teaching) are well known in the research literature (Wideen & Holborn, 1986; Zeichner, 1980). They surfaced to a certain extent also at Saint-Jean (perhaps not surprisingly given the large number of student teachers to be placed in immersion classrooms). However, Saint-Jean tries to overcome these problems by forming strong individuals with well-developed philosophies before they enter the practicum. As one faculty member told us:

> 'I know that the system is very strong and the system will shape them. Therefore, they will have to have a very strong stance when they leave here, of who they are, what they stand for, what are truly their convictions.'

In this way, students can be objective about their practicum experience and profit from contact with a diversity of models. In the words of one student:

> 'It is just examples. We are given examples of everything, and from there we judge whether it's positive or negative. It could be a negative role model also. That way we learn what kind of things we don't want to do. We evaluate and observe the effects of the different things that they do.'

Thus, the extended practicum, which is often seen as problematic in teacher education, is turned into a program strength. This is consistent with research suggesting that experiences with contrasting or conflicting models of teaching may lead to growth in student teachers' beliefs (Hollingsworth, 1989).

Simon Fraser University

Simon Fraser University is a mid- to large-sized English language university located in Burnaby, British Columbia, enrolling over 15,000 students and offering a broad range of undergraduate and graduate degrees. Established in 1965, it carries with it the recent 'history' of a new and flexible university, responsive and open to educational change. Innovative and specialized programs have always been a hallmark of the university, and among these, the Faculty of Education's program for preparing teachers, the Professional Development Program (PDP), is one of the oldest and most widely known and respected on campus and in the community at large.

Three major features characterize the PDP: (1) a differentiated staffing model, whereby master teachers designated as faculty associates are seconded from local school districts for a period of two years and work side by side with faculty members to develop and deliver the program for student teachers; (2) a significant amount of practical experience, which begins very early in the students' training and involves about six months of the 12 month program; and (3) an organizational structure whereby small groups of 28–42 students work closely with two or three faculty associates and a faculty member in modules, each with a special emphasis or theme (e.g. Elementary Generalist, Secondary Majors, Early Childhood, Diversity in Elementary Education). These features are consistent with recent calls in the research literature for the increased participation of practicing teachers in teacher education, a greater integration of theory and practice, and more attention to structural features which will contribute to the process of inducting student teachers into the profession (Goodlad, 1991; Howey & Zimpher, 1989; Tom, 1991).

Language and culture have long been the focus of attention in the PDP, with a community-based Native Teacher Education program established in the 1970s and a Multicultural module emphasizing cultural diversity in teaching established in 1980. This move toward providing alternatives in teacher education, together with the flexibility of the program's staffing model, were key factors in allowing the faculty to respond to the growing demand for French immersion teachers which was just beginning to reach British Columbia in the early 1980s.

Many conditions favoured the development of the immersion teacher education program at Simon Fraser, not the least of which was the university's willingness to recognize the use of French as an instructional language for any approved course in the calendar. This enabled the Faculty of Education to offer immersion student teachers the opportunity to take not only their practica but many of their education courses in French. In addition, the modular arrangement, by which students can work in small and cohesive groups with the same instructional team, allowed a French-speaking milieu to establish itself within an English-speaking environment. And the differentiated staffing model enabled immersion practitioners to join with faculty in preparing a special kind of second language teacher – one who teaches a second language and at the same time teaches subject matter through that language.

These practitioners, leaders in developing immersion in British Columbia, come to Simon Fraser with a high level of energy and commitment. In addition, they are generally used to working with considerable responsibility and independence in the developing terrain of French immersion in their school districts. Fortunately, the climate which receives them is well suited to their experiences and needs. Faculty associates are intimately involved in planning and delivering the program collaboratively with faculty, and their professional responsibility and expertise are highly valued. As the Director of the Program told us:

'We are not trying to teach or prove our curriculum. In fact, if anything, we want to do the exact opposite. We want very much to have the teachers' involvement in the curriculum, and this is including the faculty associates and faculty members.'

The flexibility of the program, the ongoing planning process, and orientation for new faculty associates each year create a sense of ownership and a feeling that the program is created anew. In addition, faculty associates are given considerable opportunities for professional development while they are at Simon Fraser, and they feel nurtured as individuals and professionals. They told us of many ongoing professional benefits they had gained from their experience; for example, a stronger sense of professionalism, a more abstract awareness of their pedagogy, contact with other professionals and other districts, and the motivation and incentive to inquire into what they were doing and why.

The PDP is a one-year program divided into three semesters of approximately four months each (see Table 5.2). The underlying philosophy and goals of the program are understood and shared among participants through an oral rather than written tradition: 'The goals are passed on from year to year as to what we want; it is an oral philosophy'. In addition to a child-centered orientation, key elements include learner autonomy, reflectiveness and self-analysis, achieving a proper balance between theory and practice, developing a sense of professionalism, and laying the basis for lifelong learning. These are deeply embedded in the program model and woven through the students' experiences in the three semesters.

Figure 5.2 Simon Fraser University: The professional development program

Semester 1	Semester 2	Semester 3
Blended campus and school experience	Full semester practicum	Semester of coursework (four courses)
Implemented cooperatively by faculty and faculty associates	Supervised by faculty associates	Taught by faculty, faculty associates, and instructors

The first semester is an integrated program of alternating blocks of classroom teaching and on-campus instruction aimed at developing students' knowledge and skills in both the theory and practice of teaching. Consistent with principles of adult learning, students have the opportunity to identify their own professional goals and plan for their further professional development. The intensiveness of the initial practicum experience gives students the opportunity to discover whether they want to become teachers and allows them to develop a meaningful framework for their theoretical learning, self-evaluation and improvement. Although the classroom experience appeared to be most salient when students talked to us about this semester, the words of one student suggest how personal the theory/practice integration is and how this begins to take place:

> 'Not just in the workshops and not just through the actual being in the classroom, but the whole thing put together. It had a kind of geometric progression. It started fitting in toward the middle of November. Finally things started falling into the right slots.'

The second semester is an extended practicum experience in the schools, during which students gain extensive experience in teaching in immersion classrooms. The theory/practice flow is maintained through readings students undertake as part of their work for this semester and through support provided by the faculty associate. This individual visits student teachers in the schools every seven to ten days, observes and conferences with them using a developmental supervision model, initiates readings relevant to their classwork, and responds to their journals. Daily support and supervision are provided by school associates, who are expected to serve as guides and mentors to students, observe and conference with them systematically, and participate in the evaluation process.

We spent a good part of our time observing the supervisory cycle when we visited immersion schools and thus were able to gain greater familiarity with the faculty associate's role. Overall, we found that the faculty associate managed to provide considerable help and guidance to student teachers in the technical aspects of teaching while at the same time stimulating student teachers to talk about and reflect on themselves and their teaching. The faculty associate encouraged student teachers to use specific evidence from the classroom to support what they said, stimulated them to generalize beyond the specific situation, and enabled them to go beyond their own preoccupations and consider their teaching from the point of view of the children in the class. By her systematic and frequent supervision, she appeared to provide students with a model of reflection, and above all the time and the space to engage in this process. However, we also noted that attention to technique or approach sometimes prevailed at the expense of its suitability to subject matter (e.g. group consensus required in cooperative learning versus divergent thinking appropriate to the interpretation of poetry) and that broader issues arising out of the teaching situation tended not to be discussed in the supervisory conferences.

In their final semester of the program, students undertake from 14–18 semester credit hours of academic coursework designed to enable them to build on strengths and eliminate deficiencies in their preparation for teaching. Because students had completed the extended practicum, they said they felt prepared to teach and seemed to be interested in taking courses that would help them in their future teaching assignments rather than courses of a more theoretical nature. However, they recognized that they had gained a meaningful framework for understanding their coursework and seemed to approach this with eagerness. Their work includes a required course in immersion methodology and research and a selection of courses offered in French (e.g. Methods courses tailored specifically to French immersion, Learning Assistance, Early Childhood Education, and Teaching French as a Second Language). Through these courses, they gain familiarity with research on immersion, theoretical grounding in second language learning and teaching, and a basis for integrating language and subject matter teaching. They also gain familiarity with a diversity of instructional approaches, and indeed an emphasis on the modelling of instructional strategies and techniques was apparent in all the courses we visited.

Discussion

The preparation of immersion teachers is widely discussed in the literature (Calvé, 1989; Frisson-Rickson & Rebuffot, 1986; Hébert, 1987; Lapkin et al., 1990; Obadia, 1984; Tardif, 1985). Both programs we studied attempt to address the major components of immersion teacher education we find in the literature, and they share many similarities particularly in the emphasis they place on second language and immersion pedagogy, theoretical aspects of second language learning and bilingualism, and the immersion practicum experience. However, despite their similarities, each program conceptualizes immersion teacher education in a somewhat different way, and each appears to provide a unique set of advantages when viewed from the perspective of immersion teacher education and teacher education generally. These advantages lie in the richness of the language and culture component and its integration with foundational studies at the Faculté Saint-Jean and in the nature of the extended practicum experience and differentiated staffing model at Simon Fraser University.

It should not be surprising that a program embedded in a francophone setting would provide advantages in the linguistic and cultural dimensions of immersion teacher education. However, these advantages are not only in the increased opportunities for linguistic and cultural learning and experience provided at Saint-Jean but in the kind of learning this can entail. This has been shaped primarily by the faculty who have utilized all aspects of the Saint-Jean milieu, including the institutional history and mission, their own biographies, students' varied backgrounds, the living culture of the community, and the formal program of studies, as a basis for exploring topics and issues dealing with language and culture (e.g. relationships between language and identity, language and society, language and culture, language and schooling) both formally and informally with students.

By encouraging informal dialogue about these issues and grounding them in the francophone minority reality, faculty have enabled students to gain firsthand knowledge and experience with the meaning of 'language and culture' in their own lives, in the lives of others, and in schooling and society. By tying these issues into the general foundational coursework, they have enabled students to learn about them in a more formalized, abstract fashion and have given them a basis for critically examining broader questions related to the social, moral and political dimensions of teaching, learning and schooling. The lack of consideration given to these questions in the preparation of teachers has emerged as an important issue in teacher education (Goodlad, 1991; Howey & Zimpher, 1989; Zeichner, 1987). The Faculté Saint-Jean experience provides at least one example of how one Canadian institution in a francophone setting has addressed this important aspect of teacher preparation.

Although there may be many viewpoints, the Saint-Jean conceptualization should stimulate considerable dialogue in the future as to what the linguistic, cultural and foundational components of immersion teacher education might imply and how these can be more closely integrated. Since its beginning, the goals of French immersion have been threefold: promoting French language skills, fostering more positive attitudes toward French-speaking Canadians, and promoting appreciation and understanding of francophone cultures. There is perhaps no better way to prepare future immersion teachers for fostering these goals than by giving them the opportunity to examine their own assumptions about and become more sensitized to the multiple linguistic and cultural realities of French-Canadian life.

Turning to the Simon Fraser program, we note particular advantages in its staffing model and in the nature of the extended practicum experience provided to students. A pivotal role is played by the faculty associate who establishes a close relationship with students, observes them frequently, and guides them through the varied and often overwhelming situations they encounter in the schools, ensuring that a consistent focus is placed on reflection, the integration of theory and practice, the needs of learners, technical skills of teaching, and theoretical perspectives of language learning.

In the practicum post-conferences we observed, significant attention was paid to stimulating student teachers to examine and reflect on their teaching. This enabled students to gain greater awareness of their role and helped them see their teaching from the point of view of the learner. As one student suddenly realized near the end of his post-conference: 'Moi j'étais obsédé par l'imparfait et puis j'ai oublié le vécu de l'enfant'. In the conferences we observed, attention was also paid to specific aspects of language teaching (e.g. providing context, encouraging oral activity, reinforcing oral with written language, attending to vocabulary learning) in addition to the more general aspects of teaching (e.g. lesson planning, management, cooperative learning strategies). Although this was not exploited as fully as it could have been in the conferences we saw, the Simon Fraser model appears to us to be particularly advantageous in that it can ensure that this aspect of immersion teacher preparation is systematically attended to in a real teaching context. This is important because in addition to combining subject-matter and language teaching through planned integration (e.g. Snow et al., 1989), as discussed in Chapter 3, immersion teachers must make on-the-spot decisions as to when, where and how to move in the continuum of language and subject matter teaching in response to their perceptions of children's understanding, background, motivation, and the particularities of the classroom situation.

In summary, the approach conceptualized and operationalized by each institution provides valuable guidelines for developing and improving immersion teacher education programs elsewhere. The program at the Faculté Saint-Jean addresses essential issues in language and culture, lays the groundwork for a more critical examination of fundamental issues in education, and contributes to our notion of what the substantive preparation of future immersion teachers might entail. The program at Simon Fraser University illustrates how the immersion practicum experience might be developed to encourage reflection in action (Schön, 1987) and how it could be exploited to ensure that students are systematically oriented to various aspects of immersion pedagogy within the practice teaching situation.

Each program also has other strengths; and these become particularly evident when one refers to the case study literature in teacher education. In their study of six distinctive teacher education programs in the United States, Howey & Zimpher (1989) stressed the importance of providing 'programs' of teacher education rather than collections of courses or experiences. Among the essential features in their concept of program is the presence of one or more frameworks or conceptions concerning the role of the teacher, the nature of teaching and learning, and the mission of schools, which provide direction to all aspects of the teacher education endeavor. The Saint-Jean program is illuminated by a well articulated philosophy, enabling common understandings to be built up among faculty and students and uniting all aspects of program development and faculty and student life. Discussion about this philosophy is encouraged, allowing students to examine its implications and giving them an anchor for developing their own philosophy and a basis for exploring broader issues involved in learning, teaching and schooling. The Simon Fraser program relies more on an oral rather than written philosophy, and key conceptions such as that of the student as autonomous learner and the teacher as reflective practitioner and life-long learner are shared and understood among its participants and deeply embedded in the program model.

Another important feature in the notion of program is the attention given to ethos and culture and to the socialization of future teachers. Both institutions we studied had a nurturing social and intellectual environment, with considerable affective support given to student teachers and close inter-personal and collegial relationships shared among participants. Faculty at both institutions placed great emphasis on instilling professional attitudes and preparing immersion teachers to undertake broader responsibilities in curriculum development and school-community relations. They also saw themselves as important models for their students. At Simon Fraser, modeling and discussion of teaching strategies and techniques were stressed. As one faculty member told us, 'I not only model. I stop and talk about what we have just done, and I bring in the whole metacognition aspect of it'. At Saint-Jean, modeling was seen in terms of the program's philosophy of developing the teacher as a person. Considerable emphasis was placed on human striving and challenge, achieving a balance between individual liberty and social responsibility, and congruence between one's beliefs and actions; and the kind of modeling that was considered important derived from these values.

A third important feature identified by Howey & Zimpher is shared faculty leadership in the delivery of the program. At both sites we visited, there was a strong sense of common ownership and joint responsibility among program members. Faculty and instructional staff worked as a team in planning, teaching and evaluating the program and worked actively toward curricular articulation and integration and program improvement and change. New initiatives developed by individual members were also evident, such as a thrust towards collaborative planning undertaken by some instructors at Simon Fraser and an innovative course emphasizing the role of the teacher as researcher at Saint-Jean. In addition, the differentiated staffing model at Simon Fraser, in which field-based and university-based faculty collaborate in delivering pre-service teacher education, provides a mechanism for staff renewal and helps circumvent problems of program sustenance and faculty burn-out which appear to plague many teacher education programs.

Howey & Zimpher developed a list of 14 attributes which appeared to characterize the programs they had examined. It was striking to find that the institutions we studied reflected so many of the attributes they identified (e.g. programs driven by clear conceptions of schooling/teaching; faculty coalescence around programs with distinctive qualities and symbolic titles; themes which run through the curriculum; an appropriate balance between theory and practice; student cohort groups; an integrative approach to curriculum; articulation between campus and school activities). This not only speaks well for the two institutions but also provides independent validation of Howey & Zimpher's work in different settings. Further research is now necessary to determine whether and how these characteristics contribute to program effectiveness. Based on our study, we suggest an additional important characteristic for examining programs of teacher education. This is an orientation to having students examine and discuss their own beliefs and practices as the basis for individual growth and learning, whether it is seen in the dialogue that occurs around language and culture and the broader atmosphere of critical inquiry and discourse that one finds at the Faculté Saint-Jean or by the reflection-in-action model utilized in the extended practicum at Simon Fraser University. This is consistent with some of the directions provided in an agenda for research on teacher learning and change (Kennedy, 1991) and the importance currently placed on the cognitive and personal dimensions of learning to teach (Clark, 1988; Freeman, 1991; Hollingsworth, 1989; Johnson, 1992).

While the programs we studied had many characteristics which correspond to the descriptions of distinctive programs elsewhere, our experiences at both sites left us with the impression that a true dialogue and triadic relationship among the three members of the teaching education endeavor (cooperating teacher, student teacher, and university supervisor or faculty associate) was somewhat lacking. Yet research suggests that this is an important aspect of teacher preparation (Grimmett, 1988, 1994); and there is increasing recognition of the need to involve practicing teachers as equal partners in teacher education and research (Holmes Group, 1986, 1990; Ontario Royal Commission, 1995). For immersion teacher education, this should be an especially fruitful avenue to follow, given the widely recognized need for articulating a pedagogy of immersion teaching and the central role practicing teachers play in program development.

To close, we underscore the need for institutional commitment and support that is viewed as basic to teacher education (Goodlad, 1991). It is clear that the programs we studied could not have thrived without the energetic and committed groups of individuals who collaborated in developing and delivering them or without the favorable institutional climate in which they grew. We hope that these and other institutions will continue to develop immersion teacher education programs and explore the newer reform proposals for teacher education currently being discussed in the literature.

Notes

1. This chapter is based on the article with a similar title appearing in *The Canadian Modern Language Review* (1993) 49, 446–65.
2. At the time of the CAIT/ACPI report (Frisson-Rickson & Rebuffot, 1986), several other institutions offered at least one course for immersion teachers but were not considered to have a program in immersion teacher education.

6 French Immersion Teachers and their Professional Development Needs[1]

Introduction

In a research agenda for French immersion, teacher education is identified as an area for urgent attention (Lapkin *et al.*, 1990). The professional development needs of immersion teachers are particularly important given the dual challenges of teaching a second language and teaching subject matter through this language. As well, many immersion teachers began teaching and virtually created a program for their classrooms prior to any widespread availability of immersion teacher education programs or support services. Because there was little information on the availability of in-service for immersion teachers and the kinds of programs and services that would best respond to their needs, the Canadian Association of Immersion Teachers (CAIT/ACPI) commissioned us to conduct a national survey of the professional development needs of French immersion teachers.

The survey, which was funded by the Federal Government, was designed to gather descriptive information on the pre- and in-service education of French immersion teachers and to determine their future professional development needs. It was conducted in 1992 with 2000 teachers in over 650 schools nationwide. In this chapter, we discuss the major findings, conclusions and recommendations of the survey.

Literature Review

Recent research stresses the developmental aspects of learning to teach and views teacher education as a continuum involving not only pre-service preparation but ongoing professional development throughout a teacher's career (Berliner, 1988; Freeman, 1991). Attention to immersion teacher education is especially important, given the rapid growth of the program and the wide array of knowledge and skills required for immersion teaching (Bernhardt & Schrier, 1992; Frisson-Rickson & Rebuffot, 1986; Lorenz & Met, 1989; Obadia, 1984; Snow, 1990; Tardif, 1985; Wilton *et al.*, 1984). In an earlier survey in British Columbia (Day & Shapson, 1983), over one-half of immersion teachers (60%) reported that they had not received any specialized training for teaching French immersion during their pre-service teacher certification program; and over one-half (55%) also felt they did not have adequate opportunities for in-service. In the provincial assessment of students' French language skills (Chapter 1), less than one-fourth of BC immersion teachers said that they were satisfied with the in-service they received for reading instruction in their districts (Day *et al.*, 1988).

Creative responses to the professional development needs of immersion teachers are clearly called for. Yet, we must be aware that most in-service initiatives in education generally fall short, mainly because they are delivered as one-shot workshops, often based on topics not selected by the teachers for whom they are intended, with follow-up support rarely provided (e.g. Fullan, 1991; Hunter, 1985). We need to reverse the factors which have caused in-service efforts to fail in the past. As the basis for building the content of in-service for immersion, we can turn to: the research on second language learning; teachers' practical experience from 30 years of immersion teaching; and the work of the Canadian Association of Immersion Teachers and other educators, who have identified essential components of immersion and second language teacher education (e.g. see Chapter 5).

Various themes can be drawn from the research literature to broaden our perspective on the process of in-service. One of the most important themes is the notion of collective or interactive professionalism, according to which teachers become active agents in their professional development through collegial sharing and collaboration (Fullan, 1991; Lieberman, 1986; Little, 1987). Guidelines for collaborative work are provided in Lieberman (1986) and include such features as organizational structure; having a small core of people working on the collaboration; time for collaboration; commitment; and time to share experience and build on what has been learned. A related theme is the concept of collegial research, reflection and personal inquiry as central features of professional development (Hopkins, 1987). Such inquiry can make important contributions to improving practice and generating knowledge about teaching and learning and at the same time contributes to teachers' professional growth (Cochran-Smith & Lytle, 1993; Grimmett, 1993; Hopkins, 1987; Nunan, 1992; Rudduck & Hopkins, 1985; Wells, 1994).

Research also suggests that collaboration among various stakeholders in education (e.g. universities, school districts, teacher associations, departments of education) will be needed to meet the challenges facing teacher education in the future. These perspectives form the basis of reform agendas in Ontario and the United States (e.g. Carnegie Forum on Education, 1986; Ontario Royal Commission, 1995).

In a recent survey of school districts, the Canadian Education Association found that in-service was considered the most important way that the French immersion program could be improved (Canadian Education Association, 1992). The importance of in-service is also underlined in recent work on immersion programs in other settings (e.g. Artigal, 1991). We designed the study described in this chapter to provide teachers, policymakers, and universities with a systematic information base about the current status of and priorities for in-service as perceived by immersion teachers.

Methodology

The population for the study comprised all teachers teaching in French immersion programs in all ten provinces and both territories of Canada, a number estimated to be approximately 11,700. We drew a random sample of 2000 teachers, representing 17% of the estimated population of immersion teachers across Canada. We developed a Teacher Questionnaire (in French) on the basis of input and suggestions from the Executive Committee of CAIT/ACPI, related instruments previously developed, and research literature on French immersion programs and teacher professional development.

The Teacher Questionnaire consisted of closed-ended and open-ended items. The first section sought background information about teachers' native language and place of birth, teaching experience and educational background, and specialized preparation for teaching French immersion. The second section sought information about the opportunities teachers had had for various kinds of professional development (e.g. peer coaching, workshops, courses, participation in professional committees) and asked teachers to rate the importance of these activities for their professional development in immersion and to assess their future needs in a variety of areas (e.g. methodology of second language teaching in immersion, integrating subject matter, varying teaching strategies). The third section gathered information about professional resources and support services available to immersion teachers (e.g. professional literature in French, availability of bilingual administration) and their satisfaction with these. As a final question, teachers were asked to suggest ways in which they felt that the Association should follow up the survey.

The response rates for the survey were very gratifying, with over one-half of the national sample of immersion teachers (56.1%, 1123/2000) returning questionnaires. The provincial response rates ranged from 29.7% (Québec) to 90.0% (Northwest Territories); they were close to or higher than the national response rate in all except three cases (i.e. Québec, Prince Edward Island, and the Yukon). After analyzing the survey results, we reviewed draft reports with the CAIT/ACPI Executive Committee and then prepared and submitted the final report (Day *et al.*, 1993).

Summary of Findings

The teachers of immersion

The large majority of teachers responding to the survey (81.3%) were female. Over one-half (57.7%) had French as a native language, one-third (33.5%) had English, and an additional small percentage (3.4%) had both French and English as native languages. The great majority of teachers (88.1%) were born in Canada; the remaining, in Europe (8.5%) or elsewhere (3.4%; e.g. USA, Morocco, Vietnam).

The majority of teachers (62.5%) had six years or more teaching experience; one-fourth (24.8%) specified 6–10 years and over one-third (37.7%) 11 years or more. The majority (55.5%) had five years or less teaching experience in French immersion; nearly one-third (30.7%) specified 3–5 years and one-fourth (24.8%) specified 1–2 years.

Almost all teachers had completed their post-secondary studies and received their teaching certificate in Canada (97.2% and 98.0%, respectively). The majority (78.4% and 69.2%) had taken most of their post-secondary studies and most of their teacher certification studies in French or in both French and English. Nearly one-third (30.3%) had done most of their teacher certification studies in English.

Specialized preparation for immersion teaching

Much work has been accomplished in describing key components of immersion teacher education (e.g. Calvé, 1989; Frisson-Rickson & Rebuffot, 1986; Hébert, 1987; Tardif, 1985), and efforts are being made to set appropriate linguistic standards for student teachers completing pre-service preparation for immersion. In addition, in our study of two pre-service immersion teacher education programs (see Chapter 5), we highlight the importance of providing coherent programs rather than isolated courses for preparing immersion teachers. When asked about their specialized preparation for teaching French immersion, two-thirds of respondents to this survey (67.1%) indicated that they had not received specialized preparation for teaching French immersion *during* their pre-service education (see Table 6.1). In addition, nearly one-third of respondents (30.3%) did most of their teacher certification studies in English. These results are partly due to the fact that a great many immersion teachers have taken their teacher preparation and taught in other kinds of programs before beginning teaching in immersion.

Table 6.1 Specialized preparation for immersion

	Number	Percent
During pre-service education	(*n* = 1,123)	
Yes	370	32.9
No	753	67.1
After pre-service education	(*n* = 1,096)	
Yes	335	30.6
No	761	69.4
Combined analysis	(*n* = 1,096)	
Yes, both during and after pre-service	111	10.1
Yes, during pre-service only	259	23.6
Yes, after pre-service only	224	20.4
No, neither during nor after	502	45.8

Approximately one-third of respondents (30.6%) said that they had received specialized preparation for immersion *after* their pre-service education (Table 6.1), with most mentioning university courses or pro-grams of widely differing kinds (e.g. five-day sessions; one, two, or three courses; degree programs or certificates). Overall, we found that over one-half of respondents (54.1%) had received some specialized preparation for teaching in immersion, either during or after or both during and after their pre-service education.

According to a survey of Canadian universities initiated by CAIT/ACPI (Martin *et al.*, 1993), opportunities for specialized preparation for immersion have increased in the last ten years and are now provided in 23 Faculties of Education across Canada. In a recent issue of the Association's Journal, researchers from five provinces across Canada describe some of the initiatives undertaken and opportunities provided for immersion teachers at their institutions (*Le Journal de l'Immersion Journal*, 1992). The Association should continue efforts to promote the need for specialized preparation for immersion teaching. In this way, it can help ensure that current offerings are maintained and reviewed and that further opportunities and incentives for specialized preparation for immersion teaching are provided not only in pre-service but as part of the continuing in-service development of teachers. In addition, information on currently available opportunities for specialized preparation needs to be disseminated and incentives developed to encourage immersion teachers to avail themselves of these opportunities.

Professional development

Recent research illustrates the value of conceptualizing teacher development as a life-long process, the importance of collective or interactive professionalism, and the need for various stakeholders in education to work together. In addition, in-service education is viewed as occurring through a broad and continuous range of activities.

The results of this survey indicate that workshop participation is by far the most frequent form of professional development activity experienced by immersion teachers. When asked to specify the professional development activities designed for French immersion teachers in which they had participated, the majority (60.5%) indicated that they had participated in such a workshop activity. However, only a minority (37.8% and lower) indicated that they had participated in other kinds of professional development activities, such as collaborative planning, work, or teaching in the school, district, or province; implementation of new curriculum; and mini-course or intensive course (see Table 6.2).

When asked to assess the importance of various activities, the large majority of teachers (70.8% and higher) rated almost all activities about which they were asked as being 'very important' or 'important', showing consistency with a broad view of professional development. Table 6.3 presents these activities in rank order according to the mean ratings they received. The activities rated as *most important* for professional development in immersion were:

- collaborative planning, work, or teaching in the school, district, or province;

- workshop in the district or at a conference;
- mini-course or intensive course; and
- implementation of new curriculum.

The activity rated as least important was correspondence course or telecourse.

Table 6.2 Participation in professional development activities designed for immersion teachers

Activity	Number	Percent
		(n = 1,123)
Collaborative planning, work, or teaching in the school, district, or province	396	35.3
Peer coaching	204	18.2
Mentoring	102	9.1
Self-directed professional development	211	18.8
Implementation of new curriculum	425	37.8
Teacher as researcher in the classroom	137	12.2
Workshop in the district or at a conference	679	60.5
Mini-course or intensive course	339	30.2
University course for credit or by audit	291	25.9
Correspondence course or telecourse	57	5.1
Participation in a professional committee at the local, provincial, or national level	249	22.2
Orientation session to district or province	244	21.7

The activity teachers rated as being *most important* for professional development in immersion was collaborative planning, work, or teaching; three-fifths of respondents (60.3%) rated this as 'very important' and an additional one-third (34.0%) rated this as 'important'. These results are consistent with the emphasis on teacher collaboration in the research literature. It is of note that respondents also value workshops and various other forms of in-service as important for their professional development in immersion. This suggests the need for a comprehensive approach which builds on teachers' experiences and perceived needs and for the necessary time and support for this to take place.

Table 6.3 Professional development activities in order of perceived importance

Activity	Mean rating[a]	Rank
Collaborative planning, work, or teaching in the school, district, or province	1.5	1
Workshop in the district or at a conference	1.6	2
Mini-course or intensive course	1.7	3
Implementation of new curriculum	1.7	3
Self-directed professional development	1.8	4
Peer coaching	1.8	4
Orientation session to district or province	1.9	5
University course for credit or by audit	1.9	5
Teacher as researcher in the classroom	2.0	6
mentoring	2.0	6
Participation in a professional committee at the local, provincial, or national level	2.1	7
Correspondence course or telecourse	2.5	8

[a] Based on a three-point scale, where 1 = very important, 2 = important, and 3 = not important; a lower mean rating indicates greater perceived importance.

Teachers' responses to open-ended questions asking them to comment on future directions for improving professional development and on ways they felt that CAIT/ACPI should follow up the survey echoed the ratings they gave. They wanted the Association to facilitate opportunities for meeting and exchanging ideas, workshops, and courses or mini-courses:

> Dans le passé, ce qui m'a été très profitable étaient les sessions de partage entre collègues. Je crois que plusieurs professeurs se posent les mêmes questions, mais souvent ils ont besoin d'encouragements ou de directions. On pourrait faire plus au niveau local en s'orientant vers les besoins des professeurs qui sont exprimés.

> Je propose qu'il y ait plus de rencontres entre professeurs d'immersion dans les régions. Nous nous sentons très isolés surtout quand il n'y a qu'une école d'immersion dans le territoire.

> Le mot-clé est immersion. Tous les cours offerts étaient pour le français de base. Ici . . . il me semble que personne n'a aucune idée de la différence entre l'immersion et le français de base. Ils sont traités

comme la même discipline. J'aimerais voir des cours établis spécifiquement pour les professeurs d'immersion.

Des stages intensifs offerts au cours de l'année scolaire, pendant lesquels on fera face à un problème majeur en immersion et on trouvera des solutions qui conviennent à la plupart des enseignants.

They also called for CAIT/ACPI to continue to play a more visible and active role in promoting their professional development needs and in publishing and disseminating information on various aspects of the immersion program:

Que la croissance professionnelle soit toujours promue par tout organisme qui a trait à l'immersion et que les professeurs prennent la responsabilité d'en profiter.

Certainement plus actif et plus militant, d'être plus proche des professeurs dans le sens où le contact et les correspondances sont permanents.

Promouvoir le programme dans les conseils scolaires, publicité au sujet des succès de l'immersion, plus d'emphase sur l'aspect culturel de l'apprentissage de la langue : ateliers de formation pour les professeurs dans ce domaine.

Des liens et des sentiments d'appartenance sont d'après moi primordiaux pour le moral et la satisfaction des éducateurs en immersion. Comment y arriver?

Since its inception in 1977, the Association has been promoting professional development through its annual conference (now attended by over 1000 immersion teachers and educators), the publication of a journal for teachers, and several special projects. The results of this survey provide the Association with a mandate for further work in professional development. It will be important for the Association to increase its visibility and intensify its role in promoting and providing professional development opportunities for French immersion teachers. Ministries of Education and universities need to be made more aware of the unique professional development needs of immersion teachers and should be pressured to increase their commitment and support to professional development. Courses and opportunities designed specifically for teaching subject matter in a second language are needs particular to immersion teachers which must be provided.

Immersion program issues

Immersion pedagogy and curriculum

Teachers were asked to rate their professional development needs in a variety of areas; Table 6.4 presents these areas in rank order according to the mean ratings they received. Teachers rated teaching French language arts as the area of greatest need; nearly three-fifths of teachers (57.1%) said that they had 'great need' of professional development in this area and an additional one-third (34.9%) said that they had 'some need'. Teachers also rated other areas central to immersion pedagogy as being in need of professional development (see Table 6.4). These included teaching subject

Table 6.4 Areas for professional development in order of perceived need

Area	Mean rating[a]	Rank
Teaching French language arts in immersion	1.5	1
Developing curriculum and resources	1.5	1
Teaching subject matter in immersion	1.6	2
Varying teaching strategies	1.6	2
Meeting individual student needs	1.6	2
Motivating students in immersion	1.7	3
Integrating subject matter	1.7	3
Evaluation	1.7	3
Second language acquisition in children	1.7	3
Methodology of L2 teaching in immersion	1.7	3
Research information on immersion	1.8	4
Learning assistance	1.9	5
Child development	1.9	5
Teaching the culture of francophone communities	1.9	5
Communicating with parents	2.0	6
Classroom management	2.0	6
First language acquisition in children	2.1	7
Teaching multi-level classes	2.2	8

[a] Based on a three-point scale, where 1 = great need, 2 = some need, and 3 = no need; a lower mean rating indicates greater perceived need.

matter in immersion, motivating students in immersion, integrating subject matter, second language acquisition in children, and methodology of second language teaching. While our knowledge in all of these areas has expanded considerably, we still need to clarify what distinguishes immersion pedagogy and we need much more information on classroom practices in French immersion (Calvé, 1988; Carey, 1984; Genesee, 1987; Lapkin et al., 1990; Tardif & Weber, 1987). As illustrated in Chapter 3, exploration of teacher beliefs is also a rich and necessary area for investigation (Breen, 1991; Clark, 1988; Johnson, 1992; Laplante, 1996; Richardson et al., 1991; Salomone, 1992a) and would greatly enhance the delivery of effective pre- and in-service education for immersion teachers.

The concept of teacher research, reflection, and personal inquiry has emerged as a central feature of professional development (Cochran-Smith & Lytle, 1993; Grimmett, 1993; Hopkins, 1987; Nunan, 1992; Rudduck & Hopkins, 1985; Wells, 1994). It has, in our view, exciting potential for overcoming some of the gaps in our knowledge and understanding of immersion pedagogy and, at the same time, for contributing to teachers' learning and ownership in their professional development.

An important long-term goal for CAIT/ACPI would be to undertake work on articulating more fully the distinguishing characteristics of immersion pedagogy. This could be done by exploring and reviewing teachers' writings in various publications, such as the Association's *Le Journal de l'Immersion Journal*, *The Canadian Modern Language Review*, *Contact*, *Language and Society*, and provincial publications; encouraging teachers to bring their intuitive thoughts to the surface, articulate their strategies, and write on them; and promoting and sponsoring teacher research projects in this area.

Examination of issues in communicative teaching methodology and curricular outcomes for immersion need also to be further encouraged. While much of this work more appropriately takes place in a school or district-based context, CAIT/ACPI can play a leadership role by creating a forum in its journal and yearly conference and by developing materials to assist in addressing these issues.

Materials and resources for immersion

Teachers rated developing curriculum and resources among the areas of greatest need (Table 6.4). Comments related to the need for materials and resources appropriate for immersion students were common responses to many of the survey questions. Curricular materials should offer equivalent conceptual complexity and informational content as do those materials of corresponding grade levels in the regular English program. At the same time, they should be made accessible to students who are in the process of learning their second language by improving upon available material and by assisting teachers to develop strategies for mediating between written materials and students. As curriculum development and its accompanying resources and materials are central components of a school program, extensive support for curriculum development and research is crucial if immersion is to meet the dual goals of fostering bilingualism and providing an education which is equivalent to that of the English program.

Currently all teachers, whether they are teaching in immersion or other programs, are called on to develop curriculum and to draw on a variety of resources for teaching rather than relying predominantly on textbooks. This needs time and support. While immersion teachers share responsibilities common to all teachers, they also have special challenges and face unique problems (e.g. difficulty of access to original French resources from which to develop materials, lack of availability of bilingual librarian in the school, etc.).

It will be important for CAIT/ACPI to continue to sensitize Ministries of Education, school districts, and school personnel to the need for time and support for curriculum and materials development in immersion. Collaborative networks among teachers should be encouraged including those involving the new computer technologies, so that they can share, build on their work, and develop strategies which enable students to access French language materials.

Bilingual support services

The need for bilingual support services in the effective delivery of immersion programs has been emphasized throughout the history of immersion. Over one-half of respondents to this survey indicated that they did not have access to bilingual or francophone administration or a bilingual or francophone librarian in their school (52.0% and 57.2%, respectively). And over three-fifths (62.1%) did not have access to bilingual or francophone learning assistance in their school. CAIT/ACPI has sponsored a project in the area of learning assistance in immersion (Murtagh, 1992) and should continue with its initiatives in this area. It will also be important for the Association to continue to exert pressure on ministries, school districts, and schools to provide bilingual support personnel for immersion programs. The provision of adequate support services is an area that must be attended to in the call for more systematic implementation of immersion programs. The immersion program cannot be seen as an adjunct to the regular English system; it requires the resources and support services essential to its effective operation, especially if there is a desire that it serve a broad-based constituent group of students.

Professional qualifications

Developing high levels of language proficiency in students and helping them gain an appreciation and understanding of francophone cultures are among the major goals of French immersion. Qualifications for immersion teaching should reflect these goals. Less than one-half of respondents who had pre-service preparation for teaching French immersion indicated a course in francophone culture as part of their specialized preparation (45.9%). Many respondents to the survey noted that language proficiency was an important professional qualification which the Association should work to ensure. In addition, many respondents noted the need to have opportunities to maintain and develop their French language skills and gain experience with the cultures of francophone communities across Canada and abroad. Approximately two-thirds of teachers said that they had 'great need' or 'some need' in the areas of French language and culture (65.3% and 68.2%, respectively). Among their comments were the following:

> En tant qu'anglophone, on peut toujours chercher le perfectionnement d'une langue parlée. Afin de m'aider, j'ai voyagé et j'ai suivi divers cours au Québec et en France.

> Même si je suis francophone, j'éprouve le besoin de me perfectionner. Je sens aussi que je dois demeurer informée sur ce que font les francophones.

> Nous sommes très isolés ici et il y a très peu de francophones dans la communauté. Alors le contact est essentiel pour maintenir le niveau de compétence linguistique.

> J'aurais besoin . . . de perfectionnement culturel au niveau des communautés francophones du Manitoba.

> Il faut continuer de subventionner les cours d'été et des échanges d'école, d'élèves et de professeurs pendant l'année scolaire.

It will be important for the Association to further develop policy guidelines on qualifications for immersion teaching and make this work more widely known to its members and all those concerned with immersion education. Opportunities for teachers to maintain and develop their linguistic skills and knowledge and understanding of the cultures of francophone communities in Canada and abroad should also be promoted and encouraged by the Association as part of its initiatives in immersion teacher education.

Closing Comments

Since the inception of the program, immersion teachers have played a key role in fostering bilingualism in Canada. Their commitment to this goal and to their profession and students was evident in the survey responses. The success of French immersion owes a great deal to their dedication, hard work, and inventiveness – qualities also identified as characteristic of immersion teachers in other settings (Artigal, 1991; Baker, 1993b). However, as one of the teachers in this survey reminds us, teaching in immersion is not only the concern of the classroom teacher but of all those involved in the education of students:

> L'enseignement en immersion n'est pas seulement l'affaire du professeur de la salle de classe mais de tous les gens impliqués dans l'éducation des élèves. Il faut une ambiance de support et de coopération.

Teachers' responses and comments clearly echo the research literature which conceptualizes teacher education as a continuum of life-long learning. Systematic professional development for immersion teachers must continue to be sought. Some immersion teachers are isolated, some receive more support than others, yet *all* immersion teachers need to connect. The findings of this survey can be used to help teachers establish deeper connections and expand the shared professionalism that has always been their hallmark. We expect this work will assist the Canadian Association of Immersion Teachers in developing a collective response to many of the issues in the survey and in playing a wider and more intensive role in professional development for French immersion teachers.

Notes

1. This chapter is based on the article with a similar title appearing in *The Canadian Modern Language Review* (1996) 52, 248–70.

Conclusions

Evaluation and Assessment

Our work on immersion education spans more than a decade of research in the areas of evaluation and assessment, curriculum and instruction, and teacher education. The opening section first described the context and mechanisms developed for conducting program evaluations to answer basic questions about immersion posed by individual school districts and the public. We then narrated how our work evolved to gather more broadly based information to guide instrument development and program improvement on a province-wide scale. The features critical to our evaluation approach were: providing for both summative and formative dimensions, developing partnerships (e.g. with immersion educators, school districts, and the government), tailoring results to individual district needs, and developing a mechanism for ongoing self-evaluation by districts.

A criticism of evaluation in the beginning years of immersion was the orientation toward providing summative information on student outcomes and the consequent lack of attention to curriculum, instruction, and other factors for program improvement (Stern, 1985). Working in partnership with many school districts allowed us to consider the broader provincial picture. We found it critical to inject a formative evaluation component into our work, while still ensuring responses to summative questions about student outcomes. The intent was to increase the knowledge base so that future programs might be improved and the needs for further program development clearly identified. We also made a commitment to tailor products of our studies to the needs of all participating districts and to develop an orientation toward ongoing evaluation. This was done by preparing individual district profiles so that each district had useful results for local decision-making and developing a self-evaluation handbook containing guidelines, procedures, and instruments to assist districts with ongoing evaluation of their programs in subsequent years.

As immersion programs in the province continued to grow and expand, we were faced with the challenge of developing new assessment methods and instruments to monitor their effectiveness. A critical direction taken in our work was capitalizing on the existing provincial assessment model for the mainstream English program in order to build on its experiences, mechanisms and resources, and shape them to the unique needs of immersion. This allowed us to focus on developing comprehensive French language measures for immersion students, particularly group oral proficiency and domain-referenced reading tests, and to move away from a normative approach testing a restricted set of French language skills. Entry into the provincial assessment program also further legitimized French immersion as an established educational alternative within the public school system.

With both the maturity of the program and confidence gained through favorable evaluation findings, assessment of immersion students came to interface more comfortably with the provincial assessment model for the mainstream program. With student performance on a par or above provincial averages on subject matter tests taken in English, French rather than English came to be adopted as the language of testing for subject matter achievement for pedagogical reasons. In the final part of Section 1, we described processes developed for interpreting test results when students were tested in subject matter achievement through their second language, French, and noted some of the difficulties in translating and adapting tests so that they would be linguistically suitable for immersion students but comparable in content to English program measures. Although linguistic factors were judged to limit immersion students' performance on some test items, Interpretation Panels of immersion teachers were able to weigh linguistic considerations with their experience and knowledge of the curriculum and students, and their expectations of performance, in interpreting results and making judgements on student performance. The flexibility of immersion teachers and their ability to both consider and look beyond linguistic factors in interpreting performance were noteworthy. In addition to their suggestions for curriculum, instruction, and in-service, teachers made recommendations which they felt would help students better access their knowledge in future provincial testing in French. An important corollary of these recommendations for the classroom is that ministries and school districts should provide extensive support to immersion teachers in using and developing diverse procedures for ongoing assessment of students. This is especially important in immersion in view of secondary students' perceptions that it is more difficult to gain good grades in the French than in the English program (Halsall, 1994; Lewis & Shapson, 1989).

Our experiences reinforce the need for support for ongoing and formative research to assist program development. Immersion has a unique relationship to the mainstream program in that it is inherently part of it, carrying parallel educational goals. But because of its linguistic/cultural goals, immersion is also a distinct entity engendering its own set of needs for research, evaluation and assessment. As suggested by Burns (1986), ensuring that the distinctive needs of the program are met through policies and systematic implementation procedures are critical to the continued effectiveness of the program.

In Europe, Artigal (1991) declares that the age of monolingualism is over. Baetens Beardsmore describes school models which counter 'assumptions about the monolingual norm in educational provision' and lead to diversification of language provision (Baetens Beardsmore, 1993: 1). Clyne (1991) describes a change from monolingualism to a widespread official and societal acceptance of bilingualism in Australia. Every sociocultural situation is unique, and so our experiences cannot simply be generalized to other settings. However, by providing a comprehensive narrative account of evaluation of second language programs in our province, we underline the gradual and evolutionary nature of the process and the important role researchers can play in shaping the direction of evaluation activities and suggest that countering 'the monolingual norm' should go beyond the school level to include policies and practices at all levels of program implementation.

Curriculum and Instruction

In Section 2, we presented studies on important curricular and instructional considerations for immersion education. One of the most widely discussed areas concerns improving immersion students' oral and written grammar. Many second language theorists advocate a variable curriculum model which combines less formal, experiential teaching, involving the natural, unanalyzed use of language, with more formal language teaching based on analysis and practice of the linguistic code (Allen, 1983; Stern, 1982, 1992). To date, three experimental studies in French immersion, including our study in Chapter 2 and those by Harley (1989) and Lyster (1994a), have been conducted within this curricular orientation. The results of these studies can by no means be taken as conclusive. However, they support the view that grammatical instruction can play a positive role in immersion classrooms when it is integrated within a communicatively oriented context providing for rich and varied exposure and use of the language. Results of recent classroom-based research in second language teaching also yield increasing evidence that formal instruction can be beneficial when combined with opportunities for students to experience the structures in communication and seen in a supportive role as facilitating natural language development (Ellis, 1994).

The task is to take the encouraging findings of small-scale experimental work and ensure its generalizability under more naturalistic conditions. According to Widdowson (1990a), the pedagogic relevance of research outside the classroom can only be realized by research inside the classroom. Immersion teachers should be encouraged to experiment with their own teaching of grammar, including not only systematic curricular approaches they develop but also other means they use to focus students' attention on form (e.g. Lyster, 1994b). Consistent with Widdowson's (1990a) suggestion that teaching materials should be taken as illustrative rather than prescriptive of practice, teachers should also be encouraged to experiment further with the materials developed in the experimental studies, using them as models of ways to create a dynamic interplay between formal and functional approaches, whether incorporated within the teaching of subject matter or as a focus of separate language arts classes. The extensive diagnostic information on immersion students' speech and Harley's analysis (1993) summarizing complex considerations to be taken into account in deciding the what, when and how of grammatical teaching in immersion programs are sources which teachers can use to complement their own observations and analyses of students' progress.

It is widely recognized that language has a unique place across the school curriculum in that it is both the object of knowledge and a medium through which other knowledge is acquired (Cazden, 1973; Corson, 1990). In its latter role, language is important not only as an instrument for communication but also as an instrument for thought and learning. In Chapter 3, we used a case study approach to explore how these multiple aspects of language were being addressed in the context of subject matter (i.e. science) teaching in immersion classrooms. Case studies enable us to have vicarious encounters and expand our range of experiences (Donmoyer, 1990). When readers experience a case through another's 'eyes', their range of interpretation and hence generalization is expanded. The case studies show how individual teachers actively intervene to facilitate naturalistic acquisition processes, build on the cross-lingual aspects of learning, and encourage play about language, thereby facilitating metacognition and making their classrooms a particular kind of learning community (Kramsch & McConnell-Ginet, 1992). We hope that some of the case material will accord with teachers' experiences such that it will lead them to examine their own beliefs and practices and further contribute to our knowledge and understanding of second language programs.

Consistent with growing research which stresses the intentionality and purposefulness of teachers' work, we included an investigation of teachers' beliefs as a significant component of the case studies. Our material illustrates the richness and complexity of immersion teachers' beliefs, suggesting, along with other research from immersion classrooms (Laplante, 1995, 1996; Salomone, 1992a), that they are indeed a promising resource for increasing our knowledge of immersion pedagogy, preparing teachers, and improving practice. Particularly appropriate to work in this area are qualitative methodologies from feminist and critical ethnography perspectives, which demand that we grapple openly with observer effects, admit that our truths are partial, and allow for reciprocity of perspectives (Clifford & Marcus, 1986; Lather, 1991). In this way, we can begin to address problems of speaking for and representing teachers (Alcoff, 1991; Nespor & Barylske, 1991).

Widdowson (1990b) speaks of recognizing research as a kind of discourse which will determine conditions of relevance with respect to data, and he notes quite rightly that this process of 'legitimizing partiality' is necessary to effective inquiry. In conducting this study, there was sometimes a disjuncture between our expectations and the explanations provided by teachers. One teacher's use of paraphrasing, for example, was not primarily to provide a correct model of language, as we had initially assumed, but to provide students with a mirror they could use in checking their thoughts and at the same time to promote a general learning strategy or tool that could be used in understanding French. As immersion is concerned with both language and subject matter teaching, we should at this stage of our knowledge keep our lens as wide open as possible and be wary of limiting our perspectives; otherwise, we may close off or miss some of the subtlety of teachers' interpretations.

According to Breen (1985), we will never understand classroom language learning unless we include exploration of its lesson-by-lesson significance for those who undertake it. Breen's emphasis on investigating the microclimate of the classroom and including language teachers and learners as active participants in research falls in line with more recent conceptualizations of classroom inquiry that have come to the forefront in education. These conceptualizations recognize the important role teachers and learners can play as generators of research and/or active collaborators in the research process (Clandinin & Connelly, 1986; Cole, 1989; Cole &

Knowles, 1993; Grossman, 1990; Nunan, 1992; Rudduck & Hopkins, 1985; Wells, 1994) and acknowledge that practical and formal inquiry can work together to increase our understanding of teaching and learning (Richardson, 1994).

However, while empirical inquiry is an important source for increasing our understanding of immersion, we should also remember that teaching involves values which are open to discussion and debate. Habermas (1971) stresses the importance of conversation and dialogue in the development of human understanding. In Chapter 4 we hoped to provide a basis for such dialogue by presenting some issues that should be taken into account in considering improvements to the immersion language curriculum. Recent research shows that while there are many commonalities between the perspectives of teachers and researchers in curriculum planning, there are also important differences, with researchers more influenced by current debate within their subject matter communities and teachers approaching the endeavor more with the child in mind (Prawatt, 1993). Differences within the profession are also common and were apparent in the responses to the national survey we conducted of immersion teachers. While there are many perspectives, discussion can provide the basis for exploring the many issues that arise in an educational program such as immersion, among the most important being how to reconcile creativity and convention, freedom and constraint in second language teaching (Cazden, 1992b; Widdowson, 1990a).

Teacher Education

The significant need for specialized preparation for immersion teaching is a recurrent research theme (Lapkin et al., 1990). In Section 3, we presented studies of preparatory teacher education programs and professional development for immersion teachers.

Chapter 5 contains case studies of two immersion teacher preparation programs (one in a francophone and the other in an anglophone setting) which have developed along the lines called for in recent research. The program in the francophone setting addresses essential issues in language and culture, lays the groundwork for a more critical examination of the social, moral, and political dimensions of education, and contributes to our notion of what the substantive preparation of future immersion teachers might entail. The lack of attention given to the social, moral, and political dimensions of teaching has emerged as an important issue in teacher education (Goodlad, 1991; Howey & Zimpher, 1989). This is reflected in the tendency to separate language from its social and political context in second language (Dufficy, 1993; Peirce, 1989; Pennycook, 1990) and immersion education (Bibeau, 1991; Rebuffot, 1993). The case study of this program provides us with a valuable perspective for enhancing the design of immersion teacher education to more fully embrace the complexities involved in language learning and teaching.

The program in the anglophone setting illustrates how the immersion practicum experience might be developed to encourage reflection in action (Schön, 1987) and how it could be exploited to ensure that students are systematically oriented to various aspects of immersion pedagogy. This is important because in addition to combining subject-matter and language teaching through planned integration, immersion teachers must make on-the-spot decisions as to when, where and how to move in the continuum of language and subject matter teaching in response to the particularities of their classroom situation. This recognizes the highly situation-specific nature of teaching practice and the role which an outside individual can play in evoking and challenging teachers' understandings and knowledge of general principles (Kennedy, 1991) and is especially important for immersion given the complexity of the immersion teacher's task.

The two teacher education programs illustrated by the case studies address components considered essential in immersion teacher education and display many structural features which are characteristic of exemplary pre-service programs (Howey & Zimpher, 1989). The programs share many similarities, particularly in the emphasis placed on second language and immersion pedagogy, theoretical aspects of second language learning and bilingualism, and immersion practicum experience. However, despite their similarities, each program conceptualizes and operationalizes immersion teacher education in its own unique way, with particularities of the setting, history, and individuals contributing to give each program a distinctive shape. Each therefore provides a unique set of advantages which should be instructive to other institutions that are considering introducing specialized preparatory programs for immersion teachers.

Many teachers started in immersion before the availability of specialized teacher education programs. If we wish to maximize the impact of immersion, we must be more responsive to the needs of teachers currently in immersion classrooms. In Chapter 6, we presented the results of a national survey to gain the professional development perspectives of these teachers and the role they signalled for their national association. The majority of teachers consider a range of activities and experiences as important for their professional development and rate collaboration with colleagues most highly. The survey findings indicate that the reality falls short of the ideal, suggesting a strong and continued role for the Canadian Association of Immersion Teachers.

In addition to gathering information on various aspects of professional preparation, the survey allowed us to identify major issues in immersion education which the Association should continue to address. These included immersion pedagogy and curriculum, materials and resources, bilingual support services, and professional qualifications. As is commonly recognized, professionalization is an ongoing process which is in part determined by its members' shared knowledge and their shared commitment to extend that knowledge (Pennington, 1990; Schrier, 1993). Because knowledge of immersion pedagogy lies at the heart of immersion teacher's specialized preparation, we suggest further explication of immersion pedagogy as an important area for work by the Association and point to the value of teacher research approaches as being particularly appropriate.

The concept 'teacher research' encompasses multiple meanings and involves controversial issues related to voice, power and status (Richardson, 1994). However, many teachers and researchers have worked collaboratively toward developing structures to overcome obstacles and to address areas of mutual interest and concern (Cochran-Smith & Lytle, 1993; Wells, 1994). Inter-institutional structures and relationships have also been developed by schools and universities resulting in what Lieberman calls 'an expanded view of the nature of scholarly activity' (Lieberman, 1992:8). Building even stronger collaborative structures, so that we may all learn from and further develop the immersion program, is a major orientation in the future.

When first introduced, immersion was a small controversial pilot experiment in second language learning in Canada. Over the years, it has overcome many barriers and has developed into an innovative program with significant impact on second language education internationally. There has always been an intimate relationship between immersion programs and research. In the years ahead, we expect these relationships to evolve more fully for the further benefit of second language learning and teaching.

References

Adiv, E. (1980) An analysis of second language performance in an early French immersion program: Grades 3, 4, and 5. Montreal: Instructional Services Department, The Protestant School Board of Greater Montreal.
— (1984) An analysis of oral discourse in French immersion programs. Paper presented at the Eighth Annual Convention of the Canadian Association of Immersion Teachers, Montreal, 1–3 November.
Agar, M. (1980) *The Professional Stranger. An Informal Introduction to Ethnography*. New York: Academic Press.
Alberta Education (1991) *Language of Testing Study Report*. Edmonton: Alberta Education, Student Evaluation Branch.
— (1992) *Language of Testing Study Report*. Edmonton: Alberta Education, Student Evaluation Branch.
Alcoff, L. (1991) The problem of speaking for others. *Cultural Critique*, Winter 1991–92, 5–33.
Allen, J.P.B. (1983) A three-level curriculum model for second-language education. *The Canadian Modern Language Review* 40, 23–43.
Altwerger, B., Edelsky, C. and Flores, B. (1987) Whole language: What's new? *The Reading Teacher* 41, 144–54.
Anderson, C. (1987) Strategic teaching in science. In B. F. Jones, A. Palincsar, D. Ogle, and E. Carr (eds) *Strategic Teaching and Learning: Cognitive Instruction in the Content Areas* (pp. 73–91). Elmhurst, IL: North Central Regional Educational Laboratory.
Artigal, J.M. (1991) *The Catalan Immersion Program. A European Point of View*. Norwood, NJ: Ablex.
Baetens Beardsmore, H.(ed.) (1993) *European Models of Bilingual Education*. Clevedon, England: Multilingual Matters.
Baker, C. (1993a) *Foundations of Bilingual Education and Bilingualism*. Clevedon, England: Mutilingual Matters.
— (1993b) Bilingual education in Wales. In H. Baetens Beardsmore (ed.) *European Models of Bilingual Education* (pp. 7–29). Clevedon, England: Multilingual Matters.
Barik, H.C. (1975, revised 1976) *French Comprehension Test/Level 1*. Toronto: Ontario Institute for Studies in Education. Distributed by Scholarly Book Services.
— (1978) *French Comprehension Test/Primer*. Toronto: Ontario Institute for Studies in Education. Distributed by Scholarly Book Services.
Bateson, D. *et al.* (1986) *The 1986 British Columbia Science Assessment: General Report*. Victoria, BC: Ministry of Education, Student Assessment Branch.
— (1992a) *British Columbia Assessment of Science 1991. Technical Report I: Classical Component*. Victoria, BC: Ministry of Education.

— (1992b) *British Columbia Assessment of Science Provincial Report 1991*. Victoria, BC: Ministry of Education and Ministry Responsible for Multiculturalism and Human Rights.

Berliner, D. (1988) *The Development of Expertise in Pedagogy*. Washington, DC: American Association of Colleges for Teacher Education.

Bernhardt, E. (ed.) (1992) *Life in Language Immersion Classrooms*. Clevedon, England: Multilingual Matters.

Bernhardt, E. and Schrier, L. (1992) The development of immersion teachers. In E. Bernhardt (ed.) *Life In Language Immersion Classrooms* (pp. 113–31). Clevedon, England: Multilingual Matters.

Bibeau, G. (1991) L'immersion: De la coupe aux lèvres. *Etudes de Linguistique Appliquée* 82,127–38.

Book, C., Byers, J. and Freeman, D. (1983) Student expectations and teacher education traditions with which we can and cannot live. *Journal of Teacher Education* 34, 9–13.

Bostwick, R.M. (1994) *Immersion Education International Symposium Report*. Shizuoka, Japan: Katoh Elementary School.

Breen, M. (1985) The social context for language learning – A neglected situation? *Studies in Second Language Acquisition* 7, 135–58.

— (1991) Understanding the language teacher. In R. Phillipson, E. Kellerman, L. Selinker, M. Sharwood Smith and M. Swain (eds) *Foreign/Second Language Pedagogy Research* (pp. 213–33). Clevedon, England: Multilingual Matters.

British Columbia Ministry of Education (1995) *BC Education News*, March 4.

British Columbia Royal Commission on Education (1988) *A Legacy for Learners: The Report of the Royal Commission on Education*. Victoria, BC: Queen's Printer.

Bullock Committee (1975) *A Language for Life*. London: Her Majesty's Stationery Office.

Burns, G. (1986) French immersion implementation in Ontario: Some theoretical, policy, and applied issues. *The Canadian Modern Language Review* 42, 572–91.

Buss, M. and Laurén, C. (eds) (1995) *Language Immersion: Teaching and Second Language Acquisition. From Canada to Europe*. Vaasa/Vasa: University of Vaasa.

Calvé, P. (1988) Immersion: How high will the balloon fly? Réflexions sur une aventure pédagogique. In P. Calvé (ed.) *Aspects of/de l' Immersion* (pp. 23–42). Toronto: Ontario Educational Research Council.

— (1989) Immersion teacher education: The making of a professional (mimeo).

Canadian Education Association (1992) *French Immersion Today*. Toronto: Canadian Education Association.

Canale, M. and Swain, M. (1980) Theoretical bases of communicative approaches to second language teaching and testing. *Applied Linguistics* 1, 1–47.

Cantoni-Harvey, G. (1987) *Content-area Language Instruction: Approaches and Strategies*. Reading, MA: Addison-Wesley.

Carey, S. (1984) Reflections on a decade of French immersion. *The Canadian Modern Language Review* 41, 246–59.

— (1991) The culture of literacy in majority and minority language schools. *The Canadian Modern Language Review* 47, 950–76.

Carnegie Forum on Education (1986) *A Nation Prepared: Teachers for the 21st Century* (Excerpts from the report of a task force on teaching as a profession). Washington, DC. In *The Chronicle of Higher Education*.

Cassidy, W. and Bognar, C. (1991) *More than a Good Idea: Moving from Words to Action in Social Studies*. Victoria, BC: Ministry of Education, Assessment, Examinations and Reporting.

Cazden, C. (1973) Problems for education: Language as curriculum content and learning environment. In E. Haugen and M. Bloomfield (eds) *Language as a Human Problem* (pp. 137–50). New York: Holt, Rinehart & Winston.

— (1992a) *Whole Language Plus*. New York: Teachers College Press.

— (1992b) Vygotsky, Hymes and Bakhtin: From word to utterance and voice. In C. Cazden (ed.) *Whole Language Plus* (pp. 190–207). New York: Teachers College Press.

Celce-Murcia, M. (1991) Grammar pedagogy in second and foreign language teaching. *TESOL Quarterly* 25, 459–80.

Center for Applied Linguistics (1993) *Total and Partial Immersion Language Programs in US Elementary Schools, 1993*. Washington, DC: Center for Applied Linguistics.

Chamot, A.U. and O'Malley, J.M. (1987) The cognitive academic language learning approach: A bridge to the mainstream. *TESOL Quarterly* 21, 227–47.

Channon, G. (1971) *Innovations in Teacher Education in Canada* (CTF Publication #C-71301). Ottawa: Canadian Teachers' Federation.

Clandinin, D.J. and Connelly, F.M. (1986) Rhythms in teaching: The narrative study of teachers' personal knowledge of classrooms. *Teaching and Teacher Education* 2, 377–87.

Clark, C.M. (1988) Asking the right questions about teacher preparation: Contributions of research on teacher thinking. *Educational Researcher* 17, 5–12.

Clifford, J. and Marcus, G. (1986) *Writing Culture. The Poetics and Politics of Ethnography*. Berkeley: University of California Press.

Clyne, M. (1991) Immersion principles in second language programs – research and policy in multicultural Australia. *Journal of Multilingual and Multicultural Development* 12, 55–65.

Cochran-Smith, M. and Lytle, S. (1993) *Inside Outside. Teacher Research and Knowledge*. New York: Teachers College Press.

Cole, A. (1989) Researcher and teacher: Partners in theory building. *Journal of Education for Teaching* 15, 225–37.

Cole, A. and Knowles, J. (1993) Teacher development partnership research: A focus on methods and issues. *American Educational Research Journal* 30, 473–95.

Commissioner of Official Languages (1995) *Annual Report 1994*. Canada: Minister of Supply and Services.

Cooley, W. (1983) Improving the performance of an education system. *Educational Researcher* 12, 4–12.

Corson, D. (1990) *Language Policy across the Curriculum*. Clevedon, England: Multilingual Matters.

Crandall, J. (1987) *ESL through Content-Area Instruction*. Englewood Cliffs, NJ: Prentice-Hall.

Cuevas, G. (1990) Teaching/learning mathematics and science in a language immersion setting. In E. Lorenz and M. Met (eds) *Teaching Mathematics and Science in the Immersion Classroom* (pp. 37–76). Rockville, MD: Office of Instruction and Program Development, Montgomery County Public Schools.

Cumming, A. (1989) Student teachers' conceptions of curriculum: Toward an understanding of language-teacher development. *TESL Canada Journal* 7, 33–51.

Cummins, J. (1981) The role of primary language development in promoting educational success for language minority students. In *Schooling and Language Minority Students: A Theoretical Framework* (pp. 3–79). Sacramento, CA: California State Department of Education.

Cummins, J. and Swain, M. (1986). *Bilingualism in Education*. London: Longman.

Day, E. (1993) Integrating language and science in immersion classrooms: A case study approach. Burnaby, BC: Faculty of Education, Simon Fraser University (mimeo).

Day, E. and Shapson, S. (1983) *Elementary French Immersion Programs in British Columbia. A Survey of Administrators, Teachers, and Parents. Part I: Summary of Findings; Part II: Detailed Findings*. Burnaby, BC: BC French Study, Faculty of Education, Simon Fraser University.

— (1987) Assessment of oral communicative skills in early French immersion programmes. *Journal of Multilingual and Multicultural Development* 8, 237–60.

— (1989) Provincial assessment of French immersion programmes in British Columbia. *Evaluation and Research in Education* 3, 7–23.

— (1991) *A Study of Immersion Teacher Education: Final Report*. Submitted to the Social Sciences and Humanities Research Council of Canada. Ottawa, Ontario.

Day, E., Shapson, S. and Desquins, J. (1993) *National Survey of the Professional Development Needs of French Immersion Teachers. Final Report*. Ottawa: The Canadian Association of Immersion Teachers.

Day, E., Shapson, S. and O'Shea, T. (1988) *The BC French Immersion Assessment, 1987. General Report*. Victoria: Ministry of Education, BC.

Day, E., Shapson, S. and Rivet, M.-A. (1987) *Examiner's Manual. British Columbia French Speaking Test: Grade 7*. Burnaby, BC: BC French Study, Faculty of Education, Simon Fraser University.

de Courcy, M. (1993) Making sense of the Australian French immersion classroom. *Journal of Multilingual and Multicultural Development* 14, 173–85.

Donmoyer, R. (1990) Generalizability and the single-case study. In E.W. Eisner and A. Peshkin (eds) *Qualitative Inquiry in Education* (pp. 175–200). New York: Teachers College Press.

Dufficy, P. (1993) The pedagogy of pre-service and TESOL (Teaching English to speakers of other languages) teacher education. *Journal of Education for Teaching* 19, 83–96.

Dulay, H., Burt, M. and Krashen, S. (1982) *Language Two*. New York: Oxford University Press.

Ellis, R. (1994) *The Study of Second Language Acquisition*. Oxford: Oxford University Press.

Feiman-Nemser, S. (1989) *Teacher Preparation: Structural and Conceptual Alternatives*. East Lansing, MI: The National Center for Research on Teacher Education, Michigan State University.

Fenstermacher, G.D. (1979) A philosophical consideration of recent research on teacher effectiveness. In L.S. Shulman (ed.) *Review of Research in Education, Vol. 6* (pp. 157–85). Itasca, IL: Peacock.

Folland, D. and Robertson, D. (1976) Towards objectivity in group oral testing. *English Language Teaching Journal* 30, 156–67.

Freeman, D. (1991) 'Mistaken constructs': Re-examining the nature and assumptions of language teacher education. In J. Alatis (ed.) *Georgetown University Round*

Table on Languages and Linguistics (pp. 25–39). Washington, DC: Georgetown University Press.

Frisson-Rickson, F. and Rebuffot, J. (1986) *The Training and Retraining of Immersion Teachers: Towards Establishing National Standards.* Ottawa: Canadian Association of Immersion Teachers.

Fullan, M. (1991) *The New Meaning of Educational Change.* New York: Teachers College Press.

Genesee, F. (1978) A longitudinal evaluation of an early immersion school program. *Canadian Journal of Education* 3, 31–50.

— (1983) An invited article. Bilingual education of majority-language children: The immersion experiments in review. *Applied Psycholinguistics* 4, 1–46.

— (1984) French immersion programs. In S. Shapson and V. D'Oyley (eds) *Bilingual and Multicultural Education: Canadian Perspectives* (pp. 33–54). Clevedon, England: Multilingual Matters.

— (1985) Second language learning through immersion: A review of US programs. *Review of Educational Research* 55, 541–61.

— (1987) *Learning through Two Languages.* Cambridge, MA: Newbury House.

— (1989, May) *Second language learning in school settings: Lessons from immersion.* Paper presented at the Conference on Bilingualism, Multiculturalism and Second Language Learning in Honor of Wallace Lambert, Esterel, Québec.

— (1991) L'immersion et l'apprenant défavorisé. *Etudes de Linguistique Appliquée* 82, 77–93.

Goetz, J. and LeCompte, M. (1984) *Ethnography and Qualitative Design in Educational Research.* New York: Academic Press.

Goodlad, J.I. (1991) *Teachers for Our Nation's Schools.* San Francisco: Jossey-Bass.

Goodlad, J., Soder, R. and Sirotnik, K. (1990) *Places Where Teachers Are Taught.* San Francisco: Jossey-Bass.

Graves, D. (1983) *Writing: Teachers and Children at Work.* Exeter, NH: Heinemann.

Gray, V. (1986) A summary of the elementary school evaluation of the early French immersion program in Fredericton, New Brunswick. *The Canadian Modern Language Review* 42, 940–51.

Grimmett, P. (1988) Implications of research in teaching and teacher education research for the content and delivery of teacher education programs. In G. Gilliss (ed.) *Extended Programs of Teacher Education* (pp. 38–85). Ottawa: Canadian Teachers Federation.

— (1993) Teacher research and British Columbia's curricular instructional experiment: Implications for educational policy. *Journal of Education Policy* 8, 219–39.

— (1994) Inquiring into teacher education. In M. Wideen and I. Pye (eds) *Collaborative Research in Teacher Education* (pp. 160–83). Burnaby, BC: Institute for Studies in Teacher Education, Faculty of Education, Simon Fraser University.

Grossman, P. (1990) *The Making of a Teacher. Teacher Knowledge and Teacher Education.* New York: Teachers College Press.

Guba, E.G. and Lincoln, Y.S. (1981) *Effective Evaluation.* San Francisco: Jossey-Bass.

Habermas, J. (1971) *Knowledge and Human Interests.* Boston, MA: Beacon Press.

Halsall, N. (1994) Attrition/retention of students in French immersion with particular emphasis on secondary school. *The Canadian Modern Language Review* 50, 312–33.

Harley, B. (1987a) Functional grammar in French immersion: A classroom experiment. In B. Harley, P. Allen, J. Cummins, and M. Swain (eds) *The*

Development of Bilingual Proficiency. Final Report, Vol. II (pp. 342–415). Ontario: The Ontario Institute for Studies in Education.
— (1987b) Developing and evaluating second language materials in early French immersion. *Evaluation and Research in Education* 1, 75–81.
— (1989) Functional grammar in French immersion: A classroom experiment. *Applied Linguistics* 10, 331–59.
— (1993) Instructional strategies and SLA in early French immersion. *Studies in Second Language Acquisition* 15, 245–59.
Harley, B. and Swain, M. (1977) An analysis of verb form and function in the speech of French immersion pupils. *Working Papers on Bilingualism* 14, 31–46.
— (1984) The interlanguage of immersion students and its implications for second language teaching. In A. Davies, C. Criper, and A.P.R. Howatt (eds) *Interlanguage* (pp. 291–311). Edinburgh: Edinburgh University Press.
Hébert, Y. (1987) Towards a conceptualization of teacher education for French language schools and programs in Western Canada. *The Canadian Modern Language Review* 43, 643–63.
Hollingsworth, S. (1989) Prior beliefs and cognitive change in learning to teach. *American Educational Research Journal* 26, 160–89.
Holmes Group (1986) *Tomorrow's Teachers*. East Lansing, MI: The Holmes Group.
— (1990) *Tomorrow's Schools. Principles for the Design of Professional Development Schools*. East Lansing, MI: The Holmes Group.
Hopkins, D. (1987) Teacher research as a basis for staff development. In M. Wideen and I. Andrews (eds) *Staff Development for School Improvement* (pp. 111–28). New York: Falmer Press.
Howey, K. and Zimpher, N. (1989) *Profiles of Preservice Teacher Education*. Albany, NY: State University of New York Press.
Hunter, M. (1985) What's wrong with Madeleine Hunter? *Educational Leadership* (February), 56–70.
James, J. (1980) Learner variation: The Monitor model and language learning strategies. *Interlanguage Studies Bulletin* 2, 99–111.
Jeroski, S. (1984) *The 1984 B.C. Reading Assessment. General Report*. Victoria, BC: Ministry of Education, Student Assessment Branch.
Johnson, D. (1994) Grouping strategies for second language learners. In F. Genesee (ed.) *Educating Second Language Children* (pp. 183–211). New York: Cambridge University Press.
Johnson, K. (1992) Learning to teach: Instructional actions and decisions of preservice ESL teachers. *TESOL Quarterly* 26, 507–35.
Johnson, R.K. and Swain, M. (eds) (in press) *Immersion Education: International Perspectives*. Cambridge: Cambridge University Press.
Kagan, S. (1986) Cooperative learning and sociocultural factors in schooling. In *Beyond Language: Social and Cultural Factors in Schooling Language Minority Students* (pp. 231–98). Sacramento, CA: California State Department of Education.
Kennedy, M. (1991) *An Agenda for Research on Teacher Learning*. East Lansing, MI: National Centre for Research on Teacher Learning, Michigan State University.
Kramsch, C. and McConnell-Ginet, S. (1992) (Con) textual knowledge in language education. In C. Kramsch and S. McConnell-Ginet (eds) *Text and Context: Cross-disciplinary Perspectives on Language Study* (pp. 3–25). Toronto: D.C. Heath.

Krashen, S. (1981) Bilingual education and second language acquisition theory. In *Schooling and Language Minority Students: A Theoretical Framework* (pp. 51–79). Sacramento, CA: California State Department of Education.

— (1984) Immersion: Why it works and what it has taught us. *Language and Society* 12, 61–4.

Lambert, W. (1990) Persistent issues in bilingualism. In B. Harley, P. Allen, J. Cummins, and M. Swain (eds) *The Development of Second Language Proficiency* (pp. 201–18). New York: Cambridge University Press.

Lambert, W.E. and Tucker, G.R. (1972) *Bilingual Education of Children*. Rowley, MA: Newbury House.

Lapkin, S. and Swain, M. (1984) *Second Language Maintenance at the Secondary Level. Final Report to the Carleton Board of Education*. Toronto: The Ontario Institute for Studies in Education.

Lapkin, S., Hart, D. and Swain, M. (1991) Early and middle French immersion programs: French language outcomes. *The Canadian Modern Language Review* 48, 11–44.

Lapkin, S., Swain, M. and Shapson, S. (1990) French immersion research agenda for the 90s. *The Canadian Modern Language Review* 46, 638–74.

Laplante, B. (1993) Stratégies pédagogiques et enseignement des sciences en immersion française: Le cas d'une enseignante. *The Canadian Modern Language Review* 49, 567–88.

— (1995) Teachers' beliefs and instructional strategies in science: Pushing analysis further. Paper presented at the XXIII Annual Conference of the Canadian Society for the Study of Education, Montreal (June 1995).

— (1996) Stratégies pédagogiques et représentations de la langue dans l'enseignement des sciences en immersion française. *The Canadian Modern Language Review* 52, 440–63.

Lather, P. (1991) *Getting Smart*. New York: Routledge.

Laurén, C. and Vesterbacka, S. (eds) (1990) *Language Immersion School of Vaasa/Vasa*. Vaasa/Vasa: University of Vaasa.

Le Journal de l'Immersion Journal (1992) Table ronde: Formation et perfectionnement des maîtres en immersion. 16, 9–16.

Lentz, F., Lyster, R., Netten, J. and Tardif, C. (1994) Table ronde. Vers une pédagogie de l'immersion. *Le Journal de l'Immersion Journal* 18, 15–27.

Lewis, C. and Shapson, S. (1989) Secondary French immersion: A study of students who leave the program. *The Canadian Modern Language Review* 45, 539–48.

Lieberman, A. (1986) Collaborative work. *Educational Leadership* 43, 4–8.

— (1992) The meaning of scholarly activity and the building of community. *Educational Researcher* 21, 5–12.

Lightbown, P. (1991) Getting quality input in the second/foreign language classroom. In C. Kramsch and S. McConnell-Ginet (eds) *Text and Context: Cross-Disciplinary Perspectives on Language Study* (pp. 187–97). Toronto: D.C. Heath.

Lightbown, P. and Spada, N. (1990) Focus-on-form and corrective feedback in communicative language teaching: Effects on second language learning. *Studies in Second Language Acquisition* 12, 429–48.

Lincoln, J.W. and Guba, E. (1985) *Naturalistic Inquiry*. Beverly Hills, CA: Sage.

Lindfors, J.W. (1980) *Children's Language and Learning*. Englewood Cliffs, NJ: Prentice-Hall.

Little, J.W. (1987) Teachers as Colleagues. In V.R. Koehler (ed.) *Educators' Handbook. A Research Perspective* (pp. 491–518). New York: Longman.

Long, M.H. and Porter, P.A. (1985) Group work, interlanguage talk, and second language acquisition. *TESOL Quarterly* 19, 207–28.

Lorenz, E. and Met, M. (1989) *What It Means to be an Immersion Teacher.* Rockville, MD: Office of Instruction and Program Development, Montgomery County Public Schools.

Lyster, R. (1987) Speaking Immersion. *The Canadian Modern Language Review* 43, 701–17.

— (1990) The role of analytic language teaching in French immersion programs. *The Canadian Modern Language Review* 47, 159–76.

— (1994a) The effect of functional-analytic teaching on aspects of French immersion students' sociolinguistic competence. *Applied Linguistics* 15, 263–87.

— (1994b) La négociation de la forme: Stratégie analytique en classe d'immersion. *The Canadian Modern Language Review* 50, 1–20.

MacNeil, M. (1994) Immersion programmes employed in Gaelic medium units in Scotland. *Journal of Multilingual and Multicultural Development* 15, 245–52.

Majhanovich, S. and Fish, S. (1988) Training French immersion teachers for the primary grades. An experimental course at The University of Western Canada. *Foreign Language Annals* 21, 311–20.

Majhanovich, S. and Gray, J. (1992) The practicum: An essential component in French immersion teacher education. *The Canadian Modern Language Review* 48, 682–95.

Martin, M., Obadia, A., and Rodriguez, F. (1993) *Enquête Nationale sur les Programmes de Formation en Immersion Française au Canada.* Ottawa: Canadian Association of Immersion Teachers.

McLaughlin, B. (1990) Restructuring. *Applied Linguistics* 11, 113–28.

Merriam, S. B. (1988) *Case Study Research in Education.* San Francisco: Jossey-Bass.

Miles, M.B. and Huberman, A.M. (1984) *Qualitative Data Analysis. A Sourcebook of New Methods.* Beverly Hills, CA: Sage Publications.

Millar, R. and Driver, R. (1987) Beyond processes. *Studies in Science Education* 14, 33–62.

Mohan, B. (1986) *Language and Content.* Reading, MA: Addison-Wesley.

Morrison, D. and Lee, N. (1985) Simulating an academic tutorial: A test validation study. In Y.P. Lee, A. Fok, R. Lord, and G. Low (eds) *New Directions in Language Testing* (pp. 86–92). Oxford: Pergamon Press.

Morrison, F. and Pawley, C. (1983) *Subjects Taught in French. Tenth Annual Report to the Ministry of Education, Part I.* Ottawa: Ottawa Board of Education Research Centre.

Morrow, K.E. (1979) Communicative language testing: Revolution or evolution? In C. Brumfit and K. Johnson (eds) *The Communicative Approach to Language Teaching* (pp. 143–57). London: Oxford University Press.

Murtagh, G. (1992) *Report on Resource Services in Immersion.* Ottawa: Canadian Association of Immersion Teachers.

Mussio, J. and Greer, R.N. (1980) The British Columbia Assessment Program: An overview. *Canadian Journal of Education* 5, 22–40.

National Center for Research on Teacher Education (1988) Teacher education and learning to teach: A research agenda. *Journal of Teacher Education* 39, 27–32.

National Commission for Excellence in Teacher Education (1985) *A Call for Change in Teacher Education* (No. 85-60490). Washington, DC: AACTE.

Nespor, J. and Barylske, J. (1991) Narrative discourse and teacher knowledge. *American Educational Research Journal* 28, 805–23.

Netten, J. and Spain, W. (1989) Student–teacher interaction patterns in the French immersion classroom: Implications for levels of achievement in French language proficiency. *The Canadian Modern Language Review* 45, 485–501.

Neufeld, G. (1993) Early French immersion and proficiency in English: Some long-range effects. *Language and Society* 43, 8–10.

Nunan, D. (1990) *Understanding Language Classrooms: A Guide for Teacher Initiated Action.* New York: Prentice Hall.

— (1991) Communicative tasks and the language curriculum. *TESOL Quarterly* 25, 279–95.

— (1992) *Collaborative Language Learning and Teaching.* Cambridge: Cambridge University Press.

Obadia, A. (1984) The teachers, key to the success story. *Language and Society* 12, 15–19.

Olson, P. and Burns, G. (1983) Politics, class and happenstance: French immersion in a Canadian context. *Interchange* 14, 1–16.

Ontario Royal Commission on Learning (1995) *For the Love of Learning.* Ontario: Queen's Printer.

Osborne, R. and Freyberg, P. (1985) *Learning in Science.* Auckland, NZ: Heinemann.

O'Shea, T. (1991) Achievement of French immersion students in English, reading, mathematics, and science. Burnaby, BC: Simon Fraser University, Faculty of Education (unpublished mimeo).

Pajares, M.F. (1992) Teachers' beliefs and educational research: Cleaning up a messy construct. *Review of Educational Research* 62, 307–32.

Peirce, B. (1989) Toward a pedagogy of possibility in the teaching of English internationally: People's English in South Africa. *TESOL Quarterly* 23, 403–20.

Pennington, M. (1990) A professional development focus for the language teaching profession. In J. Richards and D. Nunan (eds) *Second Language Teacher Education* (pp. 132–50). Cambridge: Cambridge University Press.

Pennycook, A. (1990) Toward a critical applied linguistics for the 1990s. *Issues in Applied Linguistics* 1, 8–28.

Prawatt, R. (1993) *Commonalities and Differences in Views about Ideal and Actual Curriculum in Six Subject Matter Domains.* East Lansing, MI: Institute for Research on Teaching, Michigan State University.

Rebuffot, J. (1993) *Le Point sur l'Immersion au Canada.* Anjou, PQ: Centre Educatif et Culturel.

Richardson, V. (1994) Conducting research on practice. *Educational Researcher* 23, 5–10.

Richardson, V., Anders, P., Tidwell, D. and Lloyd, C. (1991) The relationship between teachers' beliefs and practices in reading comprehension instruction. *American Educational Research Journal* 28, 559–86.

Robitaille, D. and O'Shea, T. (1985) *The 1985 British Columbia Mathematics Assessment: General Report.* Victoria, BC: Ministry of Education, Student Assessment Branch.

Romaine, S. (1982) *Sociolinguistic Variation in Speech Communities.* London: Edward Arnold.

Rudduck, J. and Hopkins, D. (1985) *Research as a Basis for Teaching*. London: Heinemann.

Rutherford, W. (1987) *Second Language Grammar: Learning and Teaching*. London: Longman.

Salomone, A. (1992a) Immersion teachers' pedagogical beliefs and practices: Results of a descriptive analysis. In E. Bernhardt (ed.) *Life in Language Immersion Classrooms* (pp. 9–44). Clevedon, England: Multilingual Matters.

— (1992b) Student–teacher interactions in selected French immersion classrooms. In E. Bernhardt (ed.) *Life in Language Immersion Classrooms* (pp. 97–109). Clevedon, England: Multilingual Matters.

Savignon, S. (1983) *Communicative Competence: Theory and Classroom Practice*. Reading, MA: Addison-Wesley.

— (1991) Communicative language teaching: State of the art. *TESOL Quarterly* 25, 261–77.

Schön, D. (1987) *Educating the Reflective Practitioner*. San Francisco: Jossey-Bass.

Schrier, L. (1993) Prospects for the professionalization of foreign language teaching. In G. Gunterman (ed.) *Developing Language Teachers for a Changing World* (pp. 105–23). Lincolnwood, IL: National Textbook Company.

Shafer, R., Staab, C. and Smith, K. (1983) *Language Functions and School Success*. Glenview, IL: Scott, Foresman.

Shapson, S. (1982) What about evaluating core French? *The Canadian Modern Language Review* 39, 48–55.

— (1984) Bilingual and multicultural education. In S. Shapson and V. D'Oyley (eds) *Bilingual and Multicultural Education: Canadian Perspectives* (pp. 1–13). Clevedon, England: Multilingual Matters.

Shapson, S. and Day, E. (1982) A longitudinal evaluation of an early immersion program in British Columbia. *Journal of Multilingual and Multicultural Development* 3, 1–16.

— (1984) *Evaluation Study of the Grade 3 Early and Grade 7 Early and Late French Immersion Programs in British Columbia*. Burnaby, BC: BC French Study, Faculty of Education, Simon Fraser University.

— (1988) A comparison study of early and late French immersion programs in British Columbia. *Canadian Journal of Education* 13, 290–305.

Shapson, S. and Kaufman, D. (1978) Overview of elementary French programs in British Columbia: Issues and research. *The Canadian Modern Language Review* 34, 586–603.

Sharwood Smith, M. (1981) Consciousness raising and the second language learner. *Applied Linguistics* 11, 159–68.

Shavelson, R. and Stern, P. (1981) Research on teachers' pedagogical thoughts, judgements, decisions, and behavior. *Review of Educational Research* 51, 455–98.

Sirotnik, K. (1989) *Studying the Education of Educators. Technical Report No. 2*. Seattle: Center for Educational Renewal, University of Washington.

Snow, C. (1992) Perspectives on second-language development: Implications for bilingual education. *Educational Researcher* 21, 16–19.

Snow, M. (1987) *Immersion Teacher Handbook*. Los Angeles: University of California.

— (1989) Negotiation of meaning in the immersion classroom. In E. Lorenz and M. Met (eds) *Negotiation of Meaning* (pp. 21–48). Rockville, MD: Office of Instruction and Program Development, Montgomery County Public Schools.

— (1990) Instructional methodology in immersion foreign language education. In A. Padilla, H. Fairchild and C. Valadez (eds) *Foreign Language Education. Issues and Strategies* (pp. 156–71). Newbury Park, CA: Sage Publications.

Snow, M., Met M. and Genesee, F. (1989) A conceptual framework for the integration of language and content in second/foreign language instruction. *TESOL Quarterly* 23, 201–17.

Spada, N. and Lightbown, P. (1993) Instruction and the development of questions in L2 classrooms. *Studies in Second Language Acquisition* 15, 205–24.

Staab, C. (1983) Activities to elicit specific language functions: Varying the factors of a speech event does influence the appropriate language. *The Canadian Modern Language Review* 39, 847–58.

Stake, R.E. (1978) The case study method in social inquiry. *Educational Researcher 1,* 5–8.

Stern, H.H. (1978) French immersion in Canada: Achievements and directions. *The Canadian Modern Language Review* 34, 836–54.

— (1982) French core programs across Canada: How can we improve them? *The Canadian Modern Language Review* 39, 34–47.

— (1983) *Fundamental Concepts of Language Teaching.* Oxford: Oxford University Press.

— (1985) Bilingual schooling and foreign language education: Some implications of Canadian experiments in French immersion. In J. E. Alatis and J. Staczek (eds) *Perspectives on Bilingualism and Bilingual Education* (pp. 399–422). Washington: Georgetown University Press.

— (1992) *Issues and Options in Language Teaching.* Oxford: Oxford University Press.

Strevens, P. (1977) Special purpose language learning: A perspective. *Language Teaching and Linguistics: Abstracts* 10, 145–63.

Swain, M. (1978) School reform through bilingual education: Problems and some solutions in evaluating programs. *Comparative Education Review* 22, 420–433.

— (1985) Communicative competence: Some roles of comprehensible input and comprehensible output in its development. In S. Gass and C. Madden (eds) *Input in Second Language Acquisition* (pp. 235–53). Rowley, MA: Newbury House.

— (1987) The case for focussed input: Contrived but authentic – or how content teaching needs to be manipulated and complemented to maximize second language learning. In B. Harley *et al.* (eds) *The Development of Bilingual Proficiency: Final Report. Vol. II* (pp. 317–41). Toronto: The Ontario Institute for Studies in Education.

Swain, M. and Carroll, S. (1987) The immersion observation study. In B. Harley *et al.* (eds) *The Development of Bilingual Proficiency: Final Report. Vol. II* (pp.190–263). Toronto: The Ontario Institute for Studies in Education.

Swain, M. and Lapkin, S. (1982) *Evaluating Bilingual Education: A Canadian Case Study.* Clevedon, England: Multilingual Matters.

— (1986) Immersion French in secondary schools: 'the goods' and 'the bads'. *Contact* 5, 2–9.

Tardif, C. (1985) The education of immersion teachers: Challenge of the eighties. In R. McGillivray (ed.) *More French, s'il vous plaît!* (pp. 108–15). Ottawa: Mutual Press.

— (1991) Quelques traits distinctifs de la pédagogie d'immersion. *Etudes de Linguistique Appliquée* 82, 39–51.

— Tardif, C. (1994) Classroom teacher talk in early immersion. *The Canadian Modern Language Review* 50, 466–81.

Tardif, C. and Weber, S. (1987) French immersion research: A call for new perspectives. *The Canadian Modern Language Review* 44, 68–77.

Tom, A. (1991) Stirring the embers: Reinventing the structure and curriculum of teacher education. Paper presented at the Second International Conference on Teacher Development, Vancouver, BC.

Tough, J. (1977) *The Development of Meaning. A Study of Children's Use of Language.* London: George Allen Unwin.

Vesterbacka, S. (1991) Ritualised routines and L2 acquisition: Acquisition strategies in an immersion program. *Journal of Multilingual and Multicultural Development* 12, 35–43.

Weber, S. (1991) L'immersion française: Comment plonger sans se noyer. *Etudes de Linguistique Appliquée* 82, 52–62.

Weber, S. and Tardif, C. (1991) Culture and meaning in French immersion kindergarten. In L. Malavé and G. Duquette (eds) *Language, Culture and Cognition* (pp. 93–109). Clevedon, England: Multilingual Matters.

Wells, G. (1981) *Learning through Interaction.* Cambridge, England: Cambridge University Press.

— (1991, April) Talk for learning and teaching. Paper presented at the International Convention on Language and Literacy, University of East Anglia, England.

— (1994) *Changing Schools from Within. Creating Communities of Inquiry.* Toronto: OISE Press.

Wells, G. and Chang-Wells, G.L. (1992) *Constructing Knowledge Together.* Portsmouth, NH: Heineman.

White, L. (1991) Adverb placement in second language acquisition: Some effects of positive and negative evidence in the classroom. *Second Language Research 7,* 133–61.

Widdowson, H.G. (1990a) *Aspects of Language Teaching.* New York: Oxford University Press.

— (1990b) Discourses of inquiry and conditions of relevance. In G. Alatis (ed.) *Georgetown University Round Table on Languages and Linguistics* (pp. 37–48). Washington, DC: Georgetown University Press.

Wideen, M. and Holborn, P. (1986) Research in Canadian teacher education. *Canadian Journal of Teacher Education* 11, 557–83.

Wideen, M. *et al.* (1992) *British Columbia Assessment of Science 1991. Technical Report IV: Context for Science Component.* Victoria, BC: Ministry of Education and Ministry Responsible for Multiculturalism and Human Rights.

Wilton, F., Obadia, A., Roy, R., Saunders, B. and Tafler, R. (1984) *National Study of French Immersion Teacher Training and Professional Development.* Ottawa: Canadian Association of Immersion Teachers.

Zeichner, K. (1980) Myths and realities: Field-based experiences in preservice teacher education. *Journal of Teacher Education* 31, 45–55.

— (1987) Preparing reflective teachers: An overview of instructional strategies which have been employed in preservice teacher education. *International Journal of Educational Research* 2, 565–75.

Index

1520